500 THINGS

TO DO WITH

Pantyhose

...BESIDES WEAR THEM!

500 THINGS

TO DO WITH

Pantyhose

...BESIDES WEAR THEM!

INGENIOUS AND USEFUL WAYS TO
GIVE OLD PANTYHOSE NEW LIFE

SARA LAVIERI HUNTER

FAIR WINDS
PRESS
GLOUCESTER, MASSACHUSETTS

Text © 2006 Fair Winds Press

First published in the USA in 2006 by
Fair Winds Press
33 Commercial Street
Gloucester, MA 01930

10 09 08 07 06 1 2 3 4 5

ISBN 1-59233-185-8

 Library of Congress Cataloging-in-Publication Data
Hunter, Sara.
   500 things to do with pantyhose-- besides wear them! : ingenious and
useful ways to give old pantyhose new life / Sara Lavieri Hunter.
     p. cm.
   ISBN 1-59233-185-8
   1. Panty hose craft.   I. Title. II. Title: Five hundred things to do
with pantyhose-- besides wear them.
TT699.H84 2006
745.58'4--dc22

                                                2005033788

Cover design by Howard Grossman/12E Design
Book design by Anne Gram
Printed and bound in USA

The information in this book is for educational purposes only.
It is not intended to replace the advice of a professional.

Dedication

I dedicate this book to "Teddy Reddy"
for he brought these ideas to life

Introduction: New Life for Old Hose

HAVE YOU EVER WONDERED if there was a way to recycle your old pantyhose? All of us have had piles of pantyhose with runs, snags, and holes—not to mention pantyhose that are the wrong color and the ones that no longer fit. If you're like me, those pantyhose have ended up in the trash or stuffed in a drawer in the hope of someday being able to wear that color after all or squeeze into the ones that are too small. Well, not any more, ladies! As you'll see in this book, there are literally hundreds of ways to use those old pantyhose, so clean out your drawers and get ready to be creative!

Years ago, women made use of everything and wasted nothing. When my husband was six months old, his aunt from England made him a teddy bear. It was a red bear, and his name was "Teddy Reddy." He was so well loved that his fur became worn and his stitches came loose. It was then that we discovered that he'd been stuffed with Aunt Vera's old stockings! So recycling pantyhose is not a new concept, just an expanded one.

Have you ever considered cleaning your house with old pantyhose? They make great dust cloths, and can be used instead of a sponge to clean your bath and shower. How about cooking with pantyhose? They make great pastry bags, and can also be used to strain juices and broth. There are many ways to use pantyhose for home decorating, too. They can be stuffed and used to make a wreath base or scented sachets for your drawers and linen closet. There are endless possibilities when it comes to using pantyhose for storage. Anyone with kids knows that every toy comes with a million tiny pieces that are easily lost or misplaced. What better way to keep those tiny pieces organized than in a pair of old pantyhose?

Let's face it, pantyhose aren't meant to be worn for a lifetime. That's why it's great that they're perfect for stuffing, stretching, decorating and putting to hundreds of other good uses once they've worn out their welcome as apparel. Before my daughter was born, I was a career woman and wore pantyhose to the office every day. When I decided to leave the workforce and become a stay-at-home mom, I had tons of pairs of pantyhose filling up my dresser drawers. It seemed like such a waste to throw them away! So instead, I put on my thinking cap and found zillions of ways to bring those old hose back to life. In this book, I want to share the best of those ideas with you, and I hope that you too will give your old hose a useful new life!

TABLE OF CONTENTS

PART I

Household Uses

Chapter 1.

Cleaning with Hose

As an avid housecleaner, I am constantly looking for new and innovative ways to save time and money. Pantyhose are a great alternative to sponges, dust cloths, and paper towels.

1. Wash delicates so they don't get tangled in the washer.
   Hand-washing delicates in a bathroom sink is time-consuming and tedious. It is much faster to wash them in a washing machine. However, you don't want them to get tangled and snagged in the process. Try putting your delicates inside the leg of an old pair of pantyhose and tie it at the top before placing it in the washer.

2. Polish furniture.

Rather than searching through your husband's dresser drawers for a ratty undershirt, try dusting with your old pantyhose. You can either use the seat of your hose or a leg to dust your entire house.

3. Clean your bathtub and shower.

Everyone has a gross, scummy sponge hiding under their bathroom sink. Sponges take a while to dry when there isn't adequate airflow under the sink, and they harbor bacteria. Try using a pair of old pantyhose to scrub your tub. Pantyhose dry quickly and won't hold onto harmful germs like a sponge.

4. Remove fish from a tank.

Before you clean a fish tank, scoop up your fish with a pair of old hose. Don't forget to put them in water while you're cleaning the tank!

5. Clean out lint from the dryer.

Lint traps need to be cleaned after every load or they pose a fire hazard. But it's often hard to remove all of the lint with your hand without spilling it on the laundry-room floor. Instead, use the foot of an old pair of pantyhose to clean the lint trap. The lint will be contained and won't make a mess.

6. Clean mirrors.

Have you ever cleaned a mirror with a paper towel, only to wipe it again and again to try and get rid of the fuzzy white residue it leaves on the glass? If so, try cleaning your mirrors with pantyhose and you'll be left with a clean, lint-free shine.

7. Polish your car.

There are people who take great pride in keeping their cars spotless by washing and waxing them on a regular basis. (I wish I were one of those people!) If you are, use a pair of old pantyhose to polish your car, and you'll be happy with the scratch-free shine.

8. Scrub shower tiles.

Have you ever tried to scrub the tiles above your shower while balancing on the side of the slippery tub? I have and it's no fun! Tie or wrap a bunch of old hose around the end of a broom handle and wet the hose with cleaner to wash tiles that are out of reach.

9. Line a litter box liner.

Stretch your old hose over the litter box and fill with scoopable litter. When you're ready to clean the box, simply pick up the hose and the clumps will be contained while the clean litter falls back into the box. Now, what kitty doesn't like a clean box?

10. Clean tile grout.

Cleaning tile grout can be time-consuming, back-breaking work if it's only done every few years. Make things easier on yourself by cleaning between tiles once a week with a wet pair of hose. You'll be surprised how easy it is to get down in there and wipe away the lint and dirt.

11. Install tile grout.

When installing tile grout, use a pair of wet pantyhose to wipe the excess grout off the tiles. Unlike paper towels, they hold up well even after several uses.

12. Install caulk.

Similar to working with tile grout, caulking a sink or tub can make quite a mess. Fill a bucket with water for dunking your pantyhose and use the wet hose to wipe away excess caulk.

13. Clean kitchen countertops.

Most people think that wiping their kitchen countertops with the dirty sponge from the sink after meals is sufficient. Wrong! To truly keep bacteria, dust, and dirt at bay, countertops should be thoroughly cleaned on a weekly or regular basis. Cut the leg off an old pair of hose and spray it with a good all-purpose cleaner such as Lysol Kitchen or Fantastik. Wipe down those countertops until they sparkle.

14. Hold your trash bag.

Stop your car from being "trashed" by hanging the leg of your old hose from the gear shift, stereo knob or door handle. This little trash bag can hold everything from candy wrappers to soda cans.

15. Clean appliances.

Have you ever looked closely at the sides and handle of your refrigerator, microwave or dishwasher? If you have, then you know what I'm talking about. If you haven't, go take a look and you'll be disgusted! Your appliances need to be cleaned regularly and a great way to keep them looking new is to spray some glass or kitchen cleaner on a pair of old hose and wipe those appliances down. Please don't forget to wipe the inside of your microwave!

16. Cover your bathtub drain.

It's important to keep your tub drain covered so that your valuables and small bath toys don't get sucked down. It would be very easy for a pair of earrings or Barbie shoes to go down with the bubbles! It might be difficult to stretch a section of hose across the drain, so stuff the leg of an old pair of pantyhose into the drain before you open it. Make sure all valuables and toys are accounted for before you pull out the hose.

17. Tie hangers together.

I try to avoid the hassle of using drycleaners, but it's not always possible. Make your trip more manageable by tying the hangers together with the leg of your old hose. Not only will your drop-off be more organized, it will also be easier to carry.

18. Protect yours floors.

Protect wooden floors from scratches by softening the bottoms of your chair and table legs. Cut little pieces of old hose, fold them into small circles and use a glue gun to attach them to the feet of your tables and chairs.

19. Line a waste basket.

Old pantyhose make great liners for small trash cans or baskets. Stretch the leg of your old hose into the basket and fold the end down over the top. When the basket gets full, simply remove the old hose, tie at the top and put in the garbage can.

20. Clean windows.

If you're a frequent cleaner of windows like I am, you need a cost-effective way to make those windows shine. Buying packaged wipes can be costly and they don't go very far. Spray some glass cleaner on your windows and wipe them clean with a pair of old hose. Your windows will be spotless!

21. Dust your toilet paper holder.

Yes, people notice how clean your toilet paper holder is! It takes only a second to wipe the holder clean and you can do it easily with the foot of an old pair of hose. Not only will you feel better about having a totally presentable bathroom for guests, but you will prevent dust from flying into your face when you pull paper off the roll!

22. Catch dryer lint.

I must admit that I got this idea from both my father and my grandmother. In order to keep lint from covering your shrubbery and lawn, tie the leg of your old hose to the outside dryer vent. The lint will be contained and can be easily removed.

23. Keep car lights bright and shining.

In order to make sure that your car is visible in bad weather and at night, you must keep your headlights and taillights clean. A great way to keep those lights bright is to clean them with a pair of old pantyhose and some glass cleaner.

24. Line a compost bin liner.

My grandmother has always kept a little compost bin on her kitchen countertop for scraps. Instead of using little trash bags, line the bin with a pair of old hose that stretch over the top.

25. Cover a computer keyboard.

A computer keyboard can get so dusty and is quite difficult to clean. After you've scrubbed the keys and in between them with Q-tips, cover the keyboard with a pair of old hose. The pantyhose will prevent the keyboard from getting dusty when it's not in use and will make it easier to clean in the future.

26. Cover a computer monitor.

Although a computer monitor is easier to clean than a keyboard, it's not good for it to be dust infested. Keep your monitor dust-free by covering it with a pair of old pantyhose between uses.

27. Dust your computer screen.

Computer screens are fragile and should be only cleaned with something gentle like a dust cloth. Luckily, pantyhose are soft and won't scratch the screen, so they make a perfect dust cloth!

28. Clean your car's interior.

You don't have to waste several rolls of paper towels to get your car interior squeaky clean. Just spray some Armorall on the dash and wipe it with a pair of old hose. You and your car will be glad to see the results.

29. Hang air fresheners.

Unfortunately, the new car smell doesn't last long and is eventually overpowered by the scent of stale smoke, pet dander, and old French fries. When it's time to hang those air fresheners, pantyhose can be useful. The little string that comes attached isn't always big enough to hang the freshener where you want it. Simply cut a thin strip from an old pair of hose and use it to hang the scented tree from your rearview mirror, your door handle, or hang it behind your headrest to infuse the backseat with a fresh scent.

30. Wash dishes.

Sponges harbor a lot of bacteria, so it's best not to use them to clean your dishes and flatware. Handiwipes are great because they have air holes and dry quickly, but they can be costly. Try using the leg from your pantyhose to wash your dishes. Just hang it on the faucet afterward to dry.

31. Wash hands.

A sink isn't always available when your hands need cleaning, so I always keep wipes on hand. If you don't have wipes, cut a few squares out of your pantyhose and store them in your purse with a little bottle of hand sanitizer. When your hands get dirty, wet a piece of pantyhose with sanitizer and wipe your hands clean.

32. Mop the floor.

Old rag mops don't dry quickly and get smelly over time. The new Swiffer is great but requires about five wet cloths to clean your entire kitchen floor and that is costly. If you have an old broom handle hanging around, tie several pairs of pantyhose to the end of it and use it to clean your kitchen and bathroom floors. It will not only provide your floors with a scratch-free shine, but the pantyhose will dry quickly and won't stink up your cleaning closet.

33. Dust blinds.

Blinds are great for darkening a room, but they are so hard to clean! In my experience, I have found that dust cloths are too big to really get between the blinds and the handheld cleaners for blinds don't do a great job either. The key to having clean blinds is to use a small piece of cloth and really get in there. A section of pantyhose works perfectly. Use the corners of a square of pantyhose to get into all the tight spots.

34. Clean a telephone.

Have you ever seen the news reports on the germs hiding on your telephone receiver? If you have, you know the importance of cleaning them, especially during flu season! Spray some Lysol on a section of old pantyhose and wipe your receiver, especially the mouthpiece, clean.

35. Clean your shades.

Although shades don't get as dusty as blinds do, the bottom gets dirty from being handled. Cut the foot from an old pair of pantyhose, wet it and wipe the bottom section of your shades.

36. Clean your car.

I don't know about you, but I hate finding new scratches on my car! If you want a gentle way to clean your car, tie several pantyhose legs to the end of a mop handle. Make sure that you use many pantyhose legs and completely cover the mop so that it doesn't scratch your car. It might be a good idea to cut the legs into various lengths so that you can get into every nook and cranny.

37. Clean instruments.

When my daughter started playing the recorder, I didn't really consider how I was going to clean it after each use. Then it occurred to me . . . pantyhose! If you tie a strip of pantyhose to the end of a thin straw or pencil, it will reach up inside the recorder so you can wipe it clean.

38. Clean a fish tank.

After you remove the fish from the tank, use a pair of old hose and a vinegar and water mixture to wipe down the sides and bottom of the tank.

Chapter 2.

Cooking with Hose

I realize that cooking with pantyhose may seem a little strange, but it's certainly practical! (Wash them first, of course.) They're great for kitchen storage, as you're about to find out. Use them for pastry bags, juice strainers, and gathering cheese curds.

39. Strain orange juice.

Do you love fresh-squeezed orange juice, but hate drinking the pulp? Strain the juice through the foot of your clean old pantyhose to make a smoother, easier-to-drink juice.

40. Decorate cakes.

Decorating cakes is a great way to add a special touch to any celebration, and it's not hard to do if you use the right tools. Clean pantyhose make great pastry bags when paired with couplings and decorating tips. Cut the foot off your pantyhose, snip an inch off the end, drop the decorating tip into the opening, and put the coupling on. It's a piece of cake!

41. Store lettuce for air circulation.

The problem with bagged salad is that there isn't proper airflow in the bag, so the salad starts to wilt and turn brown shortly after you open it. Put your lettuce or salad in the clean foot or leg of your pantyhose in order to provide proper air circulation.

42. Hold garlic.

Before pressing your garlic, put the head in the foot of an old pair of pantyhose so that the skins stay contained and don't fall out all over your kitchen countertop.

43. Store oranges.

Have you ever reached for an orange and ended up with the whole pile rolling onto the floor? No one likes bruised oranges! Store your oranges in the clean leg of your pantyhose so that it's easier to take just one.

44. Store onions.

Cut off the clean leg of your pantyhose and put your onions in, tying a knot after each onion. By storing your onions this way, they will not become bruised as easily, and the onion skins will remain in the hose instead of all over your produce drawer.

45. Soak beans.

The first step in cooking dried beans for soup or chili is to soak them in water. After rinsing the beans, put them in a pair of old hose, drop them into a big stock pot, cover them with water and let them soak overnight. In the morning, you can easily drain the beans by lifting the pantyhose out of the pot. The dirt will remain in the pot and not with the beans. Bon appétit!

46. Decorate cookies and brownies.

Who doesn't like cookies and brownies with a delicate dusting of powdered sugar? It dresses them up for a party, holiday or for every day. To get the right effect, you need to control the flow of powdered sugar or you'll end up with snow-covered mountain cookies! Fill the foot of your old pantyhose with powdered sugar and gently shake over the cookies for a nice, uniform design.

47. Tie recipe cards together.

Recipe boxes are bulky and can be hard to store if you don't have unlimited cabinet space. To make more space in the kitchen, take your favorite recipes, punch a hole in the top of each one and tie them together by threading a strip of old pantyhose through the holes. Hang them from a kitchen doorknob or cabinet handle for everyday access or store them with your cookbooks. This is also a great idea for a bridal shower or housewarming basket. If cooking is the theme of your gift, buy a package of nice recipe cards and write some of your favorite recipes on them before tying them together with a strip of white pantyhose.

48. Store grapefruit.

People tend to pile their fruit in one bowl on the counter where it becomes bruised and dented. If you have the space, each fruit should be stored on its own and not in a heap. Before putting away your grapefruits, put them in the leg of your old pantyhose so that they'll keep better.

49. Store clementines.

Who doesn't like clementines? I love them, not just because they're so darn cute, but because they're also deliciously sweet. Be good to your clementines and keep them breathing easy in the leg of your old pantyhose.

50. Store nectarines.

A great way to organize your fruit is to keep it on a three-tiered tray on your kitchen counter. Not only will your fruit be separated, but you will have freed up some counter space by storing it vertically. Before placing your nectarines on the tray, drop them into the leg of your old hose so that they'll keep better.

51. Carry trail mix on a hike.

I'm not a champion hiker, but I know how hungry I get after a long walk. So if you're about to embark on a hiking adventure, be sure to pack a little snack in the foot of your old hose. Mix together some trail mix, or buy some, put it in your pantyhose and tie at the top.

52. Keep ice contained when serving from a pitcher.

Serving cold beverages during the summer months can be difficult, especially at outdoor functions. Ice cubes keep drinks cold, but they seem to escape with every cup and then the pitcher gets warm. To keep your pitcher drinks cold, put a bunch of ice inside the foot of your old hose, tie it up, and float the ice bag in the pitcher. When people are pouring, they will get a nice, cold cup of lemonade or iced tea and not a pile of ice cubes, not to mention that the pitcher itself will remain cool. If the weather is especially hot, you may need to replenish the ice pouch every so often.

53. Package cookies as gifts.

During the holidays, many people gift wrap cookies in pretty cellophane bags tied with curling ribbon. Replace those expensive cellophane bags with pantyhose and you're sure to save some money. Use the foot of your old hose or even the leg (for someone really special) to wrap your cookies. Tie the top and adorn with pretty ribbon for any holiday or occasion.

54. Make a sugar shaker.

If you like to add powdered sugar to pancakes, cookies, and waffles, you need a shaker. Using a sugar shaker helps you control the flow of sugar and makes less of a powdery mess. Put some powdered sugar in a cup, stretch a section of pantyhose over the top, and put an elastic band around the hose to keep it in place. Now tip and sprinkle onto your favorite food.

55. Hang garlic.

Garlic is supposed to fend off vampires, right? Well, better to be safe than sorry! Fill the leg of your old pantyhose with garlic, twisting or knotting after you add each head and tie at the top. Hang the garlic rope wherever you think vampires might be lurking, like next to your sink window or near the fridge.

56. Crack nuts.

Everyone in my family has a giant bowl of nuts in their house at Christmas time. Nuts are full of protein and low in carbohydrates but they sure do make a mess when you crack them open. Keep your house clean and put your guests at ease by offering them an innovative way to crack their nuts. Put the nuts inside the foot of your old pantyhose before cracking them so that the shells are contained.

57. Cover the blender.

How often do you use your blender? I wanted a blender so that I could make milkshakes for my children. This, of course, was before I had children and I had no idea that they'd prefer McDonald's shakes to mine! If you don't use your blender on a regular basis, cover it with a pair of old pantyhose so that it doesn't get dusty and grimy.

58. Cover salt and pepper shakers.

Some salt and pepper shakers have giant holes that make it hard to control what you shake out. A tricky way to limit the amount of salt that comes out of a shaker is to cover it with the foot of a clean pair of pantyhose before shaking it over your plate.

59. Store parsley.

Parsley, like lettuce, needs to breathe. After washing and drying your parsley, put it in the leg of your old pantyhose before storing it in the crisper to provide better air circulation.

60. Dry herbs.

My sister loves to cook with fresh herbs and grows them herself. I, however, love to use dried herbs because they last longer. To dry herbs, put them in the leg of your old hose to let them air out. This will prevent all the leaves from falling onto your counter.

61. Store carrots.

I love being able to buy bagged carrots that are washed, cut, and ready to eat. Unfortunately, the smaller bags aren't usually resealable. Instead of leaving the bag open in the drawer, put the remaining carrots inside the leg of your old pantyhose. The carrots will have room to breathe and will stay contained.

62. Store hot cocoa packets.

I don't have enough cabinet space to house three boxes of hot chocolate, so I decided to consolidate my cocoa packets into the leg of an old pair of pantyhose. It may not be aesthetically pleasing to see my old hose in the snack cabinet, but it sure saves a lot of space!

63. Store apples.

Apples are great until they get bruised and then mushy. The produce bags that they come home in don't provide the apples with proper ventilation and they don't last very long. Once you get home, take the apples out of the plastic bag and put them in a pair of your old pantyhose. The apples will stay fresher and won't be rolling all over your counter or crisper drawer.

64. Store potatoes.

Potatoes are great but they're dirty! They grow in the ground and that filth is then transported into your house via the dirty bag they come in. Instead of reusing the dirty bag once opened or putting the remaining uncooked potatoes on your counter, put them inside the foot of your old hose. This way, you have a clean barrier between the potatoes and the counter.

65. Filter coffee.

I may appreciate an extra jolt in the morning, but I don't like coffee grinds swimming in my coffee cup. Double-straining your java ensures a great cup each and every time. Before pouring coffee into your mug or travel cup, hold a section of pantyhose over the spout to catch any unwanted grinds.

66. Store lemons or limes.

In our house, lemons and limes have to hang out for a while before I get around to using them. Store them in the leg of your old pantyhose so they'll keep better and stay fresh longer.

67. Store tea bags.

Storing three, or more, boxes of tea can be tricky if you don't have unlimited cabinet space. Consolidate your tea bags by removing them from their boxes when you get home from the grocery store and putting them in the leg of your old pantyhose. If you have flavored teas, you may want to separate them from the decaf and regular tea bags. You can put each type of tea in a separate pantyhose foot to make sure the flavors don't mingle.

68. Steep tea leaves.

My mother-in-law is from England, so she loves a good cup of tea. When I met her, I bought her some tea leaves and a nice mug, expecting her to make good use of it. Later I learned that you need something to prevent those leaves from entering your tea! Well, I finally found a way: Put some tea leaves in the foot of your old hose, drop into a mug and fill with boiling water. Tea should steep for three minutes and not a second longer!

69. Cover your sink drainer.

My sister, Suzanne, learned this the hard way! Suzanne was in charge of the dishes after dinner and would put her pearl ring on the side of the sink so it wouldn't get wet. My father gave a pearl ring to each daughter on her sixteenth birthday, so this was a special and sentimental piece of jewelry. One evening, her ring disappeared and she was broken hearted. The ring was replaced, but the lesson was learned. Cover the drain! If you don't have a stopper, stuff the leg of your old pantyhose in the drain so that you don't lose your valuables.

70. Drain pasta.

I received a terrific set of pots for my birthday one year and they came with slotted lids for draining. There's no sense in purchasing new pots if you already have decent ones, but you can use pantyhose to make your everyday pot perform two functions in one: Once your pasta is cooked, stretch a pair of old pantyhose over the top of your pot and then flip the pot to drain. Because you didn't have to use a traditional strainer, you can enjoy washing one less dish.

71. Drain vegetables.

If you cook your veggies on the stove, straining them can be a hassle unless you have a slotted spoon, a strainer or better yet…a pair of old pantyhose. Instead of using a strainer that you'll have to wash, stretch an old pair of pantyhose over the top of the pot, tip it, and let the water run through.

72. Hold herbs when making soup.

Fresh herbs add a lot of flavor to a homemade soup, but you don't want a mouthful of parsley leaves! Put your fresh herbs, like parsley, rosemary, and a bay leaf, in the foot of your pantyhose and tie at the top. When the soup is done, simply remove the herb pouch. The herbs will infuse your broth with flavor so it tastes fantastic.

73. Cover for pudding.

Whether you're making homemade or store bought pudding, you can use pantyhose to protect it while it cools. After the pudding is mixed and ready to refrigerate, put it in a bowl and cover with a piece of your old pantyhose. The pudding will cool while being protected from crumbs and other foods that might drop onto it.

74. Cover food at a picnic.

You may have prepared a gourmet meal for the office picnic, but it won't look very appetizing if there are dead flies on the serving plates! Use the seat of your old pantyhose to cover serving plates until you are ready to eat.

75. Strain curds when making cheese.

Now, I don't know anyone who makes cheese at home, but it is possible. It's important to strain the curds when making cheese and an old pair of pantyhose is perfect for the job.

76. Season your food.

Fill the leg of your pantyhose with breadcrumbs, put your chicken in and shake, shake, shake until it coats the chicken. I will warn you that this may get a little messy, so shake over the baking dish! Not only will this prevent breadcrumbs from getting all over your floor, but it will coat the bottom of the chicken so it's even tastier.

Chapter 3.

Beauty and Beyond

It doesn't have to hurt to be beautiful, ladies! Using old panty-hose for ribbons, belts, curlers, and loofahs will ease the pain inflicted on your wallets every time you buy expensive and unnecessary beauty aids.

77. Secure pigtails.

Little girls look adorable in pigtails! But ribbons can be hard to find if you don't have a fabric or craft store nearby—and they're surprisingly expensive when you do find them. When you don't have ribbons handy, cut a pair of pantyhose into strips and use neutral, black, or white hose to tie those locks up.

78. Belt your pants or a skirt.

If you're like me, you want pants and skirts to fit just right around the waist—not too snug, and not too loose. If a pair of pants or skirt didn't come with a belt, it can be hard to find one that fits perfectly. (Or you may have to rush off to work or dinner and realize halfway there that you forgot to wear a belt!) Pantyhose come in an array of neutral colors, and they stretch to fit. Cut the leg off of your pantyhose, thread it through the belt loops, and tie to fit your favorite pants or skirt.

79. Keep as emergency napkins.

I try to keep a steady supply of napkins in my car's console, but it seems like I am always running out. Cut the legs of your pantyhose into six-inch sections and keep them in the car to use as emergency napkins.

80. Tie your ponytail holders together

To keep your hair elastics organized and easy to find, cut a long strip out of your hose, insert one end through the middle of your elastics and tie the two ends together in a bow. Simply untie the bow each time you need an elastic. You can even make a pouch for ponytail holders out of the foot of your hose by filling the foot with elastics and tying a loose knot at the top.

81. Keep ears warm in winter.

Walking in cold weather is invigorating, but you need to make sure that you're dressed appropriately. Many of the hats sold today do not completely cover your ears, and you need to cover all extremities in the bitter cold. Use the leg of your old hose to wrap around your ears under your hat.

82. Keep hair away from your face.

Whether you're washing your face, exercising, or cleaning the house, you don't want your hair flopping down onto your face. Cut a strip of pantyhose to tie around your hairline to keep hair back and out of the way.

83. Cover curlers on your head.

Regardless of how tight you roll the curlers, they will loosen during the day or night. Put the foot of your old pantyhose over your head to wrap the curlers so that they don't unroll.

84. Make hair curl.

People with straight hair want curly hair. It's inevitable! There is a solution, and it's only as far away as your dresser drawer. Cut a pair of old pantyhose into strips, and tie up bunches of hair all over your head before going to bed at night. In the morning, you'll wake up with wavy hair!

85. Tie your hair up in a ponytail.

There never seems to be an elastic band around when you need one! If you're in a pinch, tie your hair back with the leg of your old pantyhose. You can tie it as tight or as loose as you want and it won't become entangled in your hair like an elastic band.

86. Make a back-scrubber for the tub and shower.

Unless you have a personal attendant, washing your back can be very difficult! Cut strips of old pantyhose and wrap them around the end of a wooden spoon to clean those hard-to-reach spots.

87. Pad your bra.

We must, we must, we must increase our bust! Not all of us were born well-endowed or are able to spend thousands of dollars to achieve the look that we want. Stuff your bra with old pantyhose, and be sure to use a neutral color that blends with your skin. It's an easy and inexpensive way to create cleavage.

88. Wear as a hairnet.

Restaurants scrap a meal when a patron discovers a hair on their plate or in their food. Your guests and family members don't want to see your hair in their food, either. Use the foot of your pantyhose to cover and hold your hair back so that your work station remains clean.

89. Ice and injury.

When you're bumped and bruised, nothing reduces swelling quite as well as a cold compress. Washcloths are too thick and actually insulate the ice, making it harder for the cold to seep through. Instead, put some ice cubes in the foot of your old pantyhose and press lightly against the injured area.

90. Separate toes when applying nail polish.

After spending so much time perfecting the nail polish on your toes, you certainly don't want to smudge them while going about your daily business. But not all of us have two hours to sit still while our nails dry! In order to separate your toes so you don't have to stay put while they dry, cut your pantyhose into little strips and put one in between each toe until your nails are completely dry.

91. Help feet absorb moisturizer.

Summer means bare feet and sandals, so smooth, sleek feet are a must! Want a surefire way to get rid of the dried skin on your heels? Massage a rich cream or Vaseline onto your feet at bedtime and wear the feet of your pantyhose to help penetration. In the morning, you'll notice a big difference!

92. Cover hair under a wig or costume.

Bobby pins don't always do the trick when it comes to keeping all of your hair tucked neatly under a wig or costume—and they're always hard to find when you're done! Cut the foot off of your pantyhose and cover your head if you want to hide the real you.

93. Wear a sweatband.

Instead of using terrycloth sweatbands, which are thick, hot, and slow to dry out, cut strips of pantyhose and tie them around your head and wrists. They will keep the sweat from dripping down your face and hands while you're exercising, and they'll dry quickly.

94. Remove eye make-up.

In order to remove all of your eye make-up, including eye shadow, eye liner, and mascara, you really need to use a remover specifically designed for this purpose. You can use a cotton ball with the cleanser, but cotton balls tend to leave lint on your eyes and tear apart halfway through the job. Try using the feet of your old pantyhose to wipe away your eye make-up because they are soft and will stay in tact. Remember to use one piece for each eye in case of infection.

95. Use to make a loofah.

Cut a pair of pantyhose into strips and tie them together in the middle to use as a loofah in the bath or shower. Use with a liquid soap or body wash to clean and exfoliate your skin. Tie a loop at the end so that you can hang it up to dry when you're done.

96. Clean ear lobes.

One of the first things I learned after getting my ears pierced is that you have to clean your holes regularly. It's perfectly fine to wear a pair of studs for a few days without removing them, but you should clean them at least once a week. Dab a piece of pantyhose with some rubbing alcohol to thoroughly clean the holes in your ears. You clean the rest of your body regularly, so why not your ears?

97. Clean your earrings.

Once you have removed your earrings to clean your holes, dab another piece of pantyhose with rubbing alcohol to clean your earrings before putting them away or back in your ears. You wouldn't want to put dirty earrings into clean ears, right?

98. Apply toner.

When I lived at home, my mother always used to tell me that I was scrubbing layers of skin off my face. I am a fanatic about keeping things clean and that includes me! Toners are gentler on the skin than many other facial cleaners. If you use toner, why not apply it gently with a small piece of pantyhose. Cut a square, roll it into a ball and soak with toner before applying it to your face.

99. Blot lipstick.

Less is always more when it comes to make-up. Feel free to use your boldest lipstick colors to jazz up an outfit, but remember to blot away the excess with a piece of old pantyhose. And use the back of that piece to wipe away lipstick that might have gotten on your teeth.

100. Stuff your shoes.

Help your shoes keep their shape by shoving your old pantyhose in them each time you put them away. This is also a great trick for shoes that are a little too big. Just shove a wad of pantyhose in the toe part and you get a comfortable, custom fit!

101. Apply perfume.

One of my favorite perfumes is Anais Anais and I love it for two reasons. First, I love the sweet smell and secondly, I love it because it was the first gift my husband ever gave me. Unfortunately, Anais Anais doesn't come in a pump bottle and it has to be applied with your finger. I'm sure that many of you have faced this predicament. A great way to dab on perfume without getting your fingers oily is to wet a small piece of pantyhose and then apply it on your neck, behind your ears, and anywhere else that should smell sweet.

102. Apply cologne.

Sometimes men don't know when to stop when putting on cologne. They think the more they put on, the better they'll smell. Wrong! My mother used to tell me that if you can smell your perfume or cologne, then it's too strong for the people around you. Try applying your cologne by adding a little to a small piece of pantyhose, and then to your skin. Let me know when the ladies begin flocking to you!

103. Keep as a travel washcloth.

Packing to go on vacation can be quite challenging, especially if you have children in tow. Everyone wants the comforts of home but no one wants to compromise for the sake of saving space. This little tip can help: Instead of packing washcloths, especially ones for your small children, use the foot of your old pantyhose to clean your faces. You can apply whatever soap or cleanser you need. Pantyhose is a great travel cloth because it dries quicker than a heavy washcloth and takes up less space in your luggage!

104. Store bath oil balls.

I love soaking in a hot soapy tub with the lights dimmed low, enjoying thirty precious minutes all to myself. For extra pampering, add a bath oil ball to your water to enrich the water and make your skin incredibly soft. A great way to store the bath oil balls is in the foot of your old hose. You can keep them in your linen closet or on the side of the tub.

105. Hang a shower caddy.

I am not a morning person, so I need all the help I can get when it comes to getting ready. It's easier to function that early when everything you need is at your fingertips. Use old pantyhose to secure a shower caddy to your shower head. This will help you keep all of your shampoo, conditioner, soap and razors together for hassle-free mornings.

106. Wrap deodorant before traveling.

Have you ever arrived at your destination and started unpacking, only to find that everything in your toiletries bag is covered with a white or clear slime? I have and it's no picnic! After you twist your deodorant and apply it, the residue from the top of the container gets moved down the side when you put the cap on. To keep this residue from getting all over everything, wrap the foot of your old panty-hose around the container before putting it in your bag.

107. Add some cheer to a holiday outfit.

Cut the leg from the hose and use glue to adhere little jingle bells to make a holiday shirt, shoes, or hat a bit more festive.

108. Hang your eye glasses.

My mother-in-law has been looking for a pretty cord so that she can hang her eyeglasses around her neck with when she's working. I told her she can find what she's looking for in her own home. Cut a strip from an old pair of pantyhose and tie it securely to the sides of your eyeglasses or sunglasses. You can decorate the hose any way you'd like or leave them plain so that they go with any outfit.

109. Make a scarf.

If you have several colored pairs of pantyhose, you could make a pretty fall or winter scarf. It won't be as warm as a wool scarf, but it would surely add a certain element of interest to your wardrobe. Cut the feet and the seats off of your old pantyhose and braid several legs together. You can make the scarf as wide as you'd like and then tie knots at the end of each leg to make fringe.

110. Wear as a watchband.

Watchbands come in several different styles and sizes, so it can be difficult to replace one that you've had for a while. Cut small strips of pantyhose, in any color that you like, and tie one strip to each side of your watch face. You can tie a simple knot around your wrist or you can tie a bow for added effect.

111. Apply pressed powder.

Pressed powder lasts quite a while, but the little applicator pad that comes with it does not. When your pressed powder puff becomes thin and frayed, replace it with a piece of pantyhose and use that to apply powder.

112. Make hair extensions.

Many people like to make drastic changes to their hairstyles but it's scary for most of us to make a permanent change when we're not completely sure about it. Here's one way to find out if you like yourself with long, straight hair. Cut strips of pantyhose, gather a small chunk of hair and tie the strips about an inch or two from the ends. Now check out your new look in the mirror. (This is also a great idea for Halloween costumes that require long hair.)

113. Make a tank top.

There was a time when we all had tube tops and wore them proudly. Thankfully, those days are long gone! If you have a tube top laying around, sew on some pantyhose shoulder straps. Cut two long strips of hose and sew each one securely to the front and back. Now you have a tank top! Lets face it, grown women look better in tank tops!

114. Make a halter top.

If you're not into tank tops, consider making your tube top into a halter top using old pantyhose. Cut two strips of pantyhose and sew one to each side of the front. Put the shirt on and then tie the two ends in a bow around the back of your neck. Fashion has never been so easy!

115. Extend your bra strap.

As women age, gravity sets in and things go downhill, if you know what I mean! Extend the life of your bras by sewing pantyhose strips to the straps as extra reinforcement. Be sure to use white or neutral hose so that you can wear them under anything.

116. Wear rings you've outgrown.

If you've ever been pregnant, you know that there comes a time when the rings must come off! No one wants to leave their wedding ring at home, much less when they're pregnant. Cut a strip of pantyhose and hang your engagement and wedding rings on it before tying it around your neck. You will still be wearing your rings, but they'll be even closer to your heart.

117. Tie jeans closed.

I know that none of you would ever admit this, but it happens to the best of us. Age is not kind! It's painful to give up a pair of jeans and buy a bigger size so that you no longer have to lie on the bed and hold your breath in to get dressed. If you're not at this point yet, consider using your old pantyhose to extend the life of your beloved blue jeans. Simply thread a strip of pantyhose through the button hole and tie tightly to the button or the first belt loop, depending on how much room you need. You may want to wear a tunic or long t-shirt so that you don't become the talk of the town!

118. Apply blush.

A lot of women prefer to use cream blush, as opposed to powdered blush. If you are one of these women, you know how quickly the applicator sponge wears out and becomes sticky and gross. Once your blush applicator is past it's prime, use pieces of pantyhose to apply your blush.

119. Remove nail polish.

Instead of using cotton balls, I use pieces of old pantyhose to remove old, chipped nail polish. The pantyhose are soft on your nails and cuticles and because they don't absorb much of the remover, more gets onto the nails.

120. Apply eye shadow.

The problem with eye shadow compacts is that the little applicators blend all the colors together. You certainly don't want to mix purple and green eye shadows together! Use a little piece of pantyhose for each eye shadow that you have. This way, the colors will remain true and you'll no longer have to keep track of all those little applicators.

121. Apply Vicks Vapo Rub.

I love this stuff but the smell drives my husband crazy. I smear so much of it onto myself that my hands, my pajamas, and my sheets reek of Vicks. To better contain the smell, I now apply the super healing cream with the foot of my old pantyhose. Cut up several pieces and keep them in your medicine cabinet next to the Vicks. Use each foot only once.

122. Apply liquid make-up.

I am a pretty natural girl, but I do like some make-up to even out my complexion now and then. Instead of rubbing foundation on with your fingers, apply it with the foot of your old pantyhose. This will help you apply a light, even coat.

123. Apply concealer.

Most concealers come with an applicator wand, but it can take hours to cover all the spots. If you are have a larger area of blemishes to cover, use the foot of your old pantyhose to apply your cover up. It is a time saver!

124. Apply calamine lotion.

I can get poison ivy by just looking at it! Next time you find yourself covered in itchy blisters, apply calamine to every spot with the foot of your old pantyhose. You will not only love the cool relief, but you won't be mopping up pink polka dots off the bathroom floor.

125. Apply shaving cream.

Using the foot of your old pantyhose will provide your legs with a smooth and uniform covering.

126. Wear as a sash.

Sashes are back, ladies! Women are tying sashes around dress pants, jeans, and even shorts. Add a quick accessory to your outfit by tying the leg of your old hose around the waist of your pants, skirt or shorts. You can tie it on the side and let the legs drape down. Just a tip: You may want to cut off those reinforced toes first.

127. Apply cold cream.

Want to avoid getting cold cream under your fingernails when you dip into that jar? Use the foot of your old pantyhose for a less messy application.

128. Remove facial bleach.

I am part Italian with the hairs to prove it! I use facial bleach every month or so to lighten the hairs on my upper lip. Once the bleach sets, you have to remove it with a washcloth and warm water. To avoid bleaching your colored towels, wet the leg of your pantyhose with warm water instead and wipe away that cream.

129. Make a neck pillow.

Little pillows are great for long car trips or for a plane ride. If you have a bad neck, like I do, you need to take extra measures to prevent your muscles from tightening up. Pick out some pretty fabric, like fleece, cotton or flannel, and cut it into two curved strips. Sew halfway around and stuff with old pantyhose before stitching up. Be sure to make the pillow small enough to fit in your carry on.

130. Fill a flattened or understuffed pillow.

Give those old toss pillows a refresh with a little pantyhose filler. Just open the pillowcase at the seam or cut a small opening and add a few pairs of pantyhose to the filling. Move the filling around until there aren't any funny bulges, close or sew the opening shut and see how it feels!

131. Wear as a strapless bra.

If you're getting ready for an event and realize that you forgot to buy a strapless bra, tightly wrap an old pair of pantyhose, or just the leg, around your bust and tie with a firm knot. Roll the knot onto the inside so it doesn't show under clothes.

132. Keep as an emergency pair of underwear.

We've all been there! You decide at the last minute to spend another night away or your child has an accident and is without a change of underwear. Simply cut the legs off of your pantyhose and use as underwear until you get home. It may not be as comfortable as a pair of Jockey's, but it'll do.

133. Wear as a girdle.

Are your jeans a little tight? Do the buttons on your jacket bulge? If so, cut the top four of five inches off a pair of control top pantyhose and wear it around your middle to help hold things in.

134. Hang a mirror.

Give your mirror a nice vintage feel using pantyhose. Add two nails or small hooks to the back of your mirror, centering one on each side. Decide where you want the top of the mirror to hang on your wall and hammer a nail a few inches above that spot. Cut off a leg or both legs of your pantyhose (depending on how heavy the mirror is), wrap it under the two nails on the back of the mirror and tie the two ends in a bow at the top. Now hang the bow on the nail and enjoy the new look.

135. Prolong the life of your soap.

Don't throw away those little shards of soap just yet. When you get down to just a few slippery pieces, place them together in the foot of your pantyhose and tie it into a secure knot. This way, the pieces won't slip out of your hands and down the drain.

136. Make an eye mask.

This is a great idea for people who work 3rd shift and sleep during the day. If you need to have a room completely dark before you fall asleep, tie a pair of dark pantyhose around your head and make sure your eyes are completely covered. Sleep tight!

137. Replace a drawstring.

If you have ever owned a pair of drawstring pants, then you know how important it is to tie them closed before washing them. If this information has arrived too late and your pants have lost their drawstring, then you can replace it with a strip of old pantyhose. Tie the strip of pantyhose to a safety pin and inch through the tunnel until it comes out the other side. Remove the safety pin and tie knots at the end of each tie so they don't sneak back into the tunnel.

138. Apply self tanner.

For a nice bronze glow without the orange palms, use a few squares of pantyhose material to apply your self tanner.

139. Apply a mud mask.

Facial masks are great for tightening pores, moisturizing or deep cleaning but who wants to dip their fingers in that goopy mixture and get it under their fingernails? For a nice even coat, use a few squares of pantyhose to apply a mud mask to the contours of your face.

Chapter 4.

Storage Solutions

The possibilities are endless! Every little thing in your house, from beads to vehicles, can be stored away in pantyhose. Get set, get ready, and get organized!

140. Store beads for jewelry-making.

Jewelry-making is all the rage these days, and you don't want expensive beads getting lost, being sucked up in the vacuum, or finding their way into little hands. If you cut the feet off your old pantyhose, you'll have individual storage bags for all of those beautiful baubles.

141. Store puzzle pieces so they aren't lost.

There is nothing more frustrating than spending hours or even days working on a huge jigsaw puzzle, only to find that the last few pieces are missing. You look in the box a million times—they *must* be in there, right? But the pieces are lost, and so is your pleasure. With a trusty pantyhose leg, this will never happen to you again! Pour all the pieces into the leg, tie it with a rubber band or twist-tie, and put the filled stocking back in the box. Puzzle-piece escapees will be a thing of the past!

142. Store loose cassette tapes.

How many times have you lost the case for one of your favorite tapes? We all associate certain songs with special memories, and we all like to be brought back to a time gone by with an old favorite. A great way to keep those musical memories safe and handy is in the leg of an old pair of pantyhose. The cassettes will stay dust-free, and you'll never be left yearning for an old favorite again!

143. Keep a bifold door shut tightly.

Keep kids and pets from getting into your closets by tying bi-fold doors closed. Take a long strip of pantyhose and tie it tightly around both doorknobs or handles.

144. Store cedar chips in your dresser drawers.

Not all of us are lucky enough to have a cedar closet to store clothing and accessories. If you want to create a cedar drawer, simply put some cedar chips in the foot of your old pantyhose and tie a knot at the top. The woody scent will filter through the fabric of the stocking, and your drawers will smell wonderful!

145. Store tennis balls.

As a former tennis player, I can tell you that there is nothing more frustrating then finding you're out of balls as you're heading to a match. Tennis balls have great bounce and, unless they're contained, they will get lost. Trying to fit a hard, plastic container into your bag can be difficult, and many of us discard the container and throw the balls into the pile of gear in the trunk. Instead, try putting your tennis balls into the leg of your pantyhose so that they'll fit into your bag and won't get lost.

146. Make a sunglasses case.

Sunglasses get thrown into purses, onto the car seat, or into the console. If not properly cared for, sunglasses become scratched, stretched, and just plain dirty. In order to keep your shades spotless and in good working order, store them in the foot of your pantyhose and keep them in a safe place.

147. Store scented pinecones.

At Christmas time, many people like to fill their homes with the scent of cinnamon and balsam. However, burning a candle or simmering potpourri is not always an option with little ones underfoot. Many nurseries and craft stores sell cinnamon- and balsam-scented pinecones that will instantly fill your house with the wonderful, warm smells of winter. After the holidays are over, store the scented pinecones in the leg of your old pantyhose so they retain their scent for next year.

148. Store Tupperware lids and bottoms.

Have you ever opened your cabinet and had twenty Tupperware containers fall on top of you? That was a regular occurrence at our house! In order to prevent this from happening at your house, put all of the lids in one pantyhose leg and the containers in another. They'll be stored safely and will be easy to retrieve!

149. Store dried herbs.

Fresh ingredients are always best, but they can leave quite a mess in your kitchen. If you're like me, food preparation cannot interfere with the need for clean! Store your dried herbs in the foot of your old pantyhose to ensure proper ventilation and, at the same time, keep your countertops clean.

150. Store yarn.

I started knitting last year and, believe me, you don't want your yarn unraveling! I was knitting my first scarf in the car on the way to Canada last summer when it unraveled all over the car floor! I managed to get it wrapped up, but I don't want to do that again. It's hard enough to do the knitting itself, never mind untangling knots in the yarn. A great way to store your yarn is in the foot of an old pair of pantyhose. The pantyhose will prevent your yarn from unraveling, and the yarn will come out easily as you're knitting.

151. Cover the kitchen mixer.

Before I discovered the many lives of old pantyhose, I used to dust my mixer every other day. It's amazing how much dust kitchen appliances gather! Instead of dusting your kitchen appliances on a regular basis, cover them with a pair of old pantyhose so that they'll remain dust-free and be ready to cook when you are.

152. Weigh down your car.

If you've ever owned a rear wheel drive car, you know how important it is to have extra weight in the trunk. Fill several pairs of pantyhose with large rocks and keep them over the wheel wells in your trunk. The added weight will help keep you from slipping and sliding and your trunk will remain clean.

153. Store mothballs and hang in your closet.

If you're looking for a way to keep moths from damaging your sweaters and other clothing items, fill a pantyhose leg with mothballs, tie at the top, and hang from your closet pole.

154. Store jewelry when traveling.

Small pieces of jewelry can easily be lost, especially when you're traveling with several accessories. Storing jewelry in a box or bag isn't a good idea when you're traveling, because the pieces can become tangled and damaged. Cut the feet from your old pantyhose and use one for each piece of jewelry. You'll find it's easy to change accessories while you're away, and they will all arrive safely home with you.

155. Neatly store wrapping paper.

Wrapping paper is quite expensive, and the most economical way to buy it is by the roll. It just so happens that this is also the hardest type of wrapping paper to store. People seldom use an entire roll for one occasion, so you're left with half a roll of wrapping paper that won't stay together no matter how quickly you roll it and tuck it in the corner. An easy way to keep that wrapping paper rolled tightly is to roll it and tie it with a strip cut from an old pair of pantyhose. You can then store all of your wrapping paper rolls in a big plastic tub, so that they're kept neat and don't get wrinkled.

156. Wrap Christmas ornaments for storage.

When my husband and I married, I began collecting Christmas ornaments from each place we visited. I thought it would be nice to remember those trips each year when we decorated our tree. I have now started a collection for our daughter, and I hope to pass down a whole collection of ornaments to her when she is living on her own and decorating her own Christmas tree. In order to do that, I need to make sure that our ornaments are packed away properly each year. Wrapping fragile ornaments in the legs of your pantyhose and placing them in a plastic container with ornament dividers will keep them from getting broken.

157. Store batteries so they stay organized.

Toys, electronics, games, and even some books now need batteries. It's amazing how much we depend on them, and we want them to be handy when we need them. A three-year-old doesn't necessarily understand why Mommy can't fix his favorite toy and make it work again! Although it might be nice to have that favorite (loud) toy disabled for a while, the screaming and whining won't make for a peaceful afternoon. Therefore, you need an easy and accessible way to store the batteries. You can arrange them by size in several old pairs of pantyhose, where they'll be easily accessible.

158. Store sewing spools.

It can be hard to find that little slit in the top of a spool of thread, so you just throw the spool into your sewing box instead of winding it properly. Days go by, and your box is opened, moved around, and things are removed and returned. Through it all, that little spool has now become unraveled . . . what a mess! Keep your spools of thread in the foot of your old pantyhose so that the thread stays wound and doesn't end up tangled in your sewing box.

159. Transport seashells from the beach.

A seashell collection is a beautiful addition to any home, but transporting those shells from the beach to your home can be tricky. No matter how many times you rinse them in the ocean, you will always find sand in your beach bag or trunk. Although you may want to live at the beach, you don't want to bring the beach home with you! After rinsing the shells, put them in the foot of your pantyhose to keep the sand contained and your bag and car sand-free.

160. Store paper clips.

Paper clips are never there when you need them! They get lost or fall into hard-to-reach places. Whether you work at an office or at home, a great way to store paper clips is in the foot of an old pair of pantyhose.

161. Store hair accessories when traveling.

It seems that I always find lost hair accessories hiding in a luggage compartment months—or even years—after I packed them. It's essential to have the right hair accessories, and losing one could ruin an entire outfit. Am I right, ladies? Place all of your hair accessories in the foot of your pantyhose and tie a knot at the top to keep all of them together.

162. Store recycled plastic bags.

Plastic bags can be used for all sorts of things, from cleaning out litter boxes to sharing and distributing home grown vegetables. Instead of trying to pile all those bags under the sink, store them in the leg of an old pair of pantyhose and stash it in a kitchen cabinet. You'll be able to fit several inside of one leg, and they will be easily accessible.

163. Wrap picture frames when moving.

After moving several times, I have learned to pack like a pro! One of the things I've learned is that it's a waste of money to buy that expensive packing paper. It's basically newspaper without print. Instead, use your old hose to wrap fragile items like picture frames. You can put each frame in the seat of your old hose, wrap the legs around it, and tie them together so that the wrapping doesn't come loose.

164. Store all of your other pantyhose and knee-highs.

Pantyhose and knee-highs can take up quite a lot of space in your lingerie drawer, not to mention the fact that knee-highs don't always stay in pairs. When you're already running late for work or an appointment, the last thing you want to be doing is tearing apart your lingerie drawer to find a matching knee-high or a decent pair of hose. Wrap your matching knee-highs in pairs, folding one inside of the other, and store them with your pantyhose in the leg of an old pair of hose. You'll be saving time because you won't be wasting valuable time searching for the missing knee-highs, and your hose will be easy to find inside of your drawer.

165. Store spare buttons.

Every shirt, sweater, and pair of pants comes with spare buttons, and keeping track of them is not easy. You may start out with the best of intentions, storing all of the buttons in one place. However, it's impossible to store all of the buttons in one place if you don't have a good place to store them. Snip off the foot of your pantyhose, sew some elastic around the top, and store all of your spare buttons inside. You will not only have provided your hose with a new life, but given your buttons a snug pouch to call home.

166. Store glitter-coated pinecones.

During the holidays, it's always nice to add a little sparkle to your holiday table, Christmas tree, and even your window boxes. Glitter-coated pinecones make the perfect accent and can be used for years to come. Unfortunately, the glitter often falls off the pinecones, and they lose some of that appeal-and make quite a mess. Storing the pinecones in the leg of your pantyhose will not only keep the glitter from being scattered, but will also keep the pinecones from getting broken in storage.

167. Store your eyeglasses.

Are you tired of fumbling around for a dusty pair of eyeglasses on your bedside table? If so, put your eyeglasses inside the foot of an old pair of pantyhose. This will keep your glasses clean and prevent them from getting scratched.

168. Stuff a box when shipping fragile items.

Shipping fragile items can be expensive and time-consuming if you're scrambling for package fillers. Without Styrofoam packing peanuts at your disposal, you may be at a loss. However, have you considered filling a package with your old pantyhose? Just to make sure no one looks at you funny for doing so, cut your old hose into strips and use them to stuff the package. The recipients will be none the wiser!

169. Fill pill bottles to protect your pills.

Have you ever gotten a headache while traveling, only to discover that all your Motrin pills were crushed from shaking around too much in the container? Use a strip from an old pair of pantyhose to fill the top of the pill bottle so your medications stay in tact.

170. Store used scouring pads.

It takes just a little scrubbing with a S.O.S. pad to get my pans clean. I hate to throw them away afterward and waste an entire scouring pad, but I hate blue scum on my sink even more! A great way to keep the slightly used pads handy for future use is to wrap them in the foot of your old pantyhose. The pad will be able to dry out quickly and the blue scum will stay in the hose and not on your counter.

171. Store fishing bait.

My Dad used to take me fishing down at the brook to catch trout. I won't tell you about the one that got away, but I will give you a tip on how to store bait. Half the fun of going fishing is digging for night crawlers the night before and storing them in dirt so they stay nice and yummy for the fish. Fill the foot of your old hose with dirt and store the worms inside and don't forget to tie the top! The worms will be able to breathe, but not escape.

172. Store kindling wood.

One thing I learned from having three Boy Scout brothers and a father who was involved with Boy Scouts is that you need kindling to build a fire. A great way to store kindling wood is in the leg of your old pantyhose. Kindling can make a mess on your hearth without pantyhose to keep the little chips contained.

173. Wrap utensil bundles for a party.

The last thing you want to worry about during a party is whether everyone has the proper utensil to eat with. Plan ahead and organize the flatware into bundles. Once you have a head count, wrap a fork, spoon and knife inside of a napkin for each guest and tie with a strip of pantyhose. You can color coordinate the pantyhose with other party decorations so that your utensil bundles blend into the party theme. For example, black hose for Halloween parties and navy for the 4th of July.

174. Pack a can of cold soda.

Whether you're traveling, hiking or just going for a walk, I'm sure that you don't want to quench your thirst with a warm soda. Am I right? If so, put a cold pack in the foot of your old hose, rest the soda on top of the cold pack and tie a loop for a handle. It's a convenient way to carry your soda and to keep it cold.

175. Store flowers while they dry.

I have saved every flower that my husband has ever given me and drying them is no easy task. If you don't want to save stems or an entire bouquet, cut the flowers and place them in the leg of your old pantyhose. The flowers will dry and you can then make potpourri or arrange them in a keepsake box with some scented oil.

176. Store plastic cups.

If you're headed to a picnic, throw some plastic cups inside the leg of your old pantyhose and tie at the top. The cups will stay clean and can be removed one at a time.

177. Store hardware.

I have gone to great lengths to organize our toolbox and the only thing that truly seems to work is to separate all the little pieces and store them in their own pantyhose bag. Using the feet of your old pantyhose, make separate storage pouches for your screws, nails, nuts, and bolts. Tie a knot at the top of each bag to keep them contained.

178. Hold your keys.

Instead of fiddling with a ring every time you need to add or remove a key, simply tie your keys to a small strip of pantyhose. Each time you need to make a change, just untie the knot.

179. Store tissues.

I am always looking for clean tissues in my purse and it's often hard to find one. The little purse packs don't close properly and tissues seem to escape into the dark unknown (a.k.a. the bottom of my purse!). Place some tissues inside the foot of your old pantyhose and tie the top—they'll be easy to spot and will stay clean.

180. Store cotton squares.

I like to keep my routine somewhat on track when I'm traveling, especially my bedtime routine. I use cotton squares to apply toner after washing my face at home and using a piece of toilet tissue from a hotel room doesn't cut it. Using the foot of an old pair of pantyhose is a great way to transport cotton squares to and from home. The cotton squares will stay clean and will remain in tact.

181. Store lipsticks.

I rarely wear lipstick, partly because I don't feel like digging through my purse to find some. I probably have at least three lipsticks hiding in my purse right now! A great way to keep your lipsticks easily accessible is to store them together in the foot of your old pantyhose. This might also prevent them from staining your purse if the cap happens to come loose.

182. Make a mini-sewing kit.

Most women don't carry huge purses that can accommodate an entire sewing kit, so storing emergency mending tools like safety pins and a needle and thread can be difficult. Use the foot of your old pantyhose to make a little mending kit of your own. Inside the foot, place a safety pin, needle, and spool of thread so that you're not left hanging in the breeze!

183. Store Q-tips.

My husband is very picky about several things, his Q-tips being one of them! I always keep a fresh supply on hand for traveling so he'll never run out. Keep Q-tips clean by storing them in the foot of your old hose before placing them in your toiletries bag.

184. Store sequins and other small craft supplies.

It's not often that I use sequins, but my daughter loves to glue them on her Hello Kitty jewelry box. Sequins are not only hard to glue, but they're also hard to pick up! Keep your sequins and other tiny craft supplies contained in the foot of your old pantyhose and take out only what you need. This way, they will stay put until you need them.

185. Store golf balls.

I am not a golfer, but I imagine that keeping track of those balls can be difficult. A golf bag is quite tall and, short of tipping it upside down and shaking it out, finding lost balls is probably impossible. Store your golf balls in the leg of your old pantyhose and then tie the hose to the top of your bag and hang inside. This way, the golf balls will be contained and readily available. You can even store your golf tees in a separate leg of hose!

186. Tie a MP3 player around your waist.

I love walking to music because it takes my mind off the exercise and gets me moving to the beat! Unfortunately, my MP3 player didn't come with a clip so I tie it around my waist when I go out to walk. Use the wide section, like the seat, of your pantyhose to form a little pouch for your player and tie tightly around your waist.

187. Store fishing flys.

You don't have to be an avid fisherman to know the importance of bait. Fish are highly attracted to brightly colored feathers called "flys." Store your fishing fly in the foot of your old pantyhose and store it in your tackle box.

188. Store fishing hooks.

If you don't want to lug a tackle box to the riverbank, put your fishing hooks inside the foot of your old hose and tie the foot to your fishing pole. Just be sure to watch where they swing.

189. Tie your Christmas tree to your car.

It never fails! Every year, it's either a blizzard or it's 15 degrees outside when we go to pick out our Christmas tree. By the time we pick one out, it's dark out and we fumble around trying to tie the tree to our roof. Never fear, pantyhose are here! They are soft and strong enough to secure a pine tree to your roof. Lay down an old blanket before you put the tree on the roof and then make a rope out of your old pantyhose to tie it down.

190. Hang a mail basket.

My husband loves to leave piles of mail, bills and notes for himself all over the kitchen counter. I used to threaten throwing the piles away if he didn't take care of them. After about seven years of marriage, I found a solution. I bought a medium sized wicker basket to hang on the wall by the office stairs so that he could put all of his bills and mail in the basket when it arrives instead of on the counter. You can hang the basket on a nail with a strip of neutral hose so that it stays secure and hangs right where you want it.

191. Store rolls of film.

Film tends to sit on my kitchen counter for weeks before I take it to be developed. A great way to keep those undeveloped rolls from falling off the counter or getting lost is to store them in a leg of old pantyhose. Once you're ready to have the film developed, tie the top of the pantyhose and transport the film to the developer in this handy little sack.

192. Secure a pool cover.

Have you ever seen milk jugs hanging from your neighbor's pool in the winter? It's a great idea to keep the pool cover from slipping into the pool during the cold weather months. Tie water filled jugs to your pool cover with your old pantyhose this winter.

193. Store take-out menus.

Most of us have a collection of take-out menus jammed into the drawers and corners of our kitchens. To store them neatly, you can either store the take-out menus inside the leg of your old hose or you can cut a strip from the leg of your hose and tie the menus together. Whichever way you choose, make a loop at the top so that you can hang them inside a kitchen cabinet.

194. Secure your trunk.

If you want to transport something that's a little too big for the trunk and you can't find those bungee cords with the hooks on the end, use a pair of pantyhose to tie down the trunk door and keep it from blocking your view out the rear window.

195. Store jingle bell ornaments.

Jingle bell ornaments make a lot of noise and can easily fall or roll out of a bag. Store all of your jingle bells inside the leg of your old pantyhose and tie tightly at the top. You can then store them inside your ornament box.

196. Store baseballs.

A pantyhose leg is the perfect place to store baseballs and transport them to and from the field.

197. Store raquet balls.

Raquet ball is a great game and a great way to stay in shape. The plastic tube that the balls come in can take up a lot of space in your bag, so store the balls inside the leg of your old pantyhose to save yourself some space.

198. Hold Band-Aids in your purse.

We go through a lot, and I mean a lot, of Band-Aids in our house! My daughter hasn't really learned that Band-Aids are for bleeding and not for decoration, but we're working on it. In the meantime, I always keep a fresh supply of character Band-Aids in my purse. A great way to store them is to put them in the foot of your pantyhose so they don't get scattered all over the bottom of your bag.

199. Cover an umbrella.

Most umbrellas come with a cover, but they're very hard to put on. To protect your umbrella when it's not in use or to keep a wet umbrella from getting everything else wet, store yours in the leg of your old pantyhose.

200. Store mouse bait.

We have a rodent problem in our shed. Catching them in traps may not be the most humane thing to do, but I have to do something and killing mice with peanut butter doesn't seem that cruel to me. Fill the foot of your old hose with peanut butter, or Decon if you want to really kick 'em where it counts, and set up a little picnic on the shed floor.

201. Fill in spaces around the air conditioner.

When you mount an air conditioner in a window, you not only have to secure it with screws and wooden sticks, but you need to fill in the edges to keep the bugs out. Use pairs of old pantyhose to shove between your window and the air conditioner to seal it off.

202. Make a candy dish cover.

We usually buy wrapped candy, but sometimes like to keep a candy dish out for holidays. In order to make sure that our cat doesn't eat the chocolate M&M's and get poisoned, we cover the dish overnight. You can do this by putting your candy dish in the foot or leg of your clean pantyhose.

203. Cover shoes.

I don't have a shoe closet, so my shoes are stored neatly in rows, but in several levels, on the bottom of my closet. Shoes touch the ground and therefore, are very dirty. I don't want my dirty sneakers sitting on my Italian mules! Store your shoes in the legs of your old pantyhose so that the dirt from the bottom of one pair doesn't get onto the top of another pair.

204. Store drumsticks.

It's not as if there is a pouch on the side of a drum!

205. Hang cedar chips in a closet.

I love the smell of cedar— it keeps everything in the closet smelling fresh. Fill the foot of your old pantyhose with cedar chips, tie a knot at the top and then tie to your closet pole. You can control how scented your closet will be by the number of cedar chips you use.

206. Tote your laundry.

If you have to go to the Laundromat, smaller loads are easier to manage. I used to pack a huge duffle bag with my entire wardrobe, drag it across the street and sit there for hours waiting for it to be done. To get out of there quickly, shove a small load of whites in a pair of old pantyhose. Be sure to put the hose in the cycle too. That way, you can use the clean hose to carry your clean clothes home.

207. Store car information.

It's important to always have your registration in your car in the event that you get stopped or get into trouble. Along with your registration, you may want to keep records of car repairs and routine maintenance receipts. Keep all of your car information in the leg of your old pantyhose and keep it in the glove compartment.

208. Use as a coupon holder.

Who doesn't like to save money? Keep all of your coupons stored in the foot of your old pantyhose and you'll be able to find them quickly when it's time to check out.

209. Hold spare change.

I am always scrounging for change at the bottom of my purse. Simplify the search by keeping your change in the foot of your hose and keeping your bills in your wallet. For quick access to change at a drive-through or toll booth window, keep an extra pouch of coins in the car.

210. Carry ice.

The ice buckets in the hotel rooms are always too small, especially if you're having a few guests over and want to mix up some drinks. The leg of your pantyhose works great for transporting extra ice to your room.

211. Store shades.

When you move from house to house, you will probably need to change window shades. It's a good idea to save your old ones because you never know when you'll need them again. Store your old shades in a leg of pantyhose. They'll stay tightly rolled and clean so you can use them again someday.

212. Store blueprints.

Whether you're an architect or a future homeowner, a pantyhose leg is the perfect home for your blueprints. The drawings will stay rolled inside and won't get dirty when you transport them.

213. Bring coins to the bank.

Have you ever tried to carry twenty rolls of coin? It's impossible to get them out of the house, never mind to the bank! If you like to roll your own coins, carry the rolls to the bank inside the leg of your old pantyhose. If you prefer to have the bank roll and count your loose change, carry your coins to the bank in the leg of your old pantyhose.

214. Store artwork.

Now, I don't suggest doing this when you're presenting your portfolio to somebody! If you're looking for a place to store your masterpieces, roll them up and store them in the legs of your old pantyhose.

215. Store posters.

If you like to change your wall decorations like you change your underwear, you need a place to store the posters once they've had their time on your wall of fame. You can easily fit a few posters in the leg of your old pantyhose so they stay rolled and wrinkle free.

216. Store girls' hair accessories.

Since my daughter was about one year old, I have always put cute barrettes—and now hair bands and elastics—in her hair. As a baby girl grows into a toddler, preschooler, and so on, her hair becomes thicker, so the adorable baby hairclips that you bought in every color when she was one won't hold her hair when she turns two, and you have to buy more. I can only imagine how many hair accessories we'll have when she is a teenager! I needed a way to store these accessories, because we've outgrown every girly box we've found. So I cut the leg off my pantyhose and now have plenty of room for even *more* hair accessories!

217. Store Legos.

Trying to keep track of Legos is perhaps the most difficult toy-related task a parent might have. Legos are small enough to get sucked up in the vacuum, fall into a crevice, or get buried in the dust bunnies under a bed. When you've finished all but one part of a Bionicle creature, you don't want to be missing the last piece! If you store all of the Legos in the foot or leg of an old pair of pantyhose, you'll never be left with a partially assembled warrior again!

218. Store Lincoln Logs.

It's wonderful to see my daughter playing with the same toys that I grew up with. If you're familiar with Lincoln Logs, you know how big the box is. It's not practical to store toys in the boxes they come in because they take up too much space. A great way to store these logs is in the leg of your old pantyhose. You'll probably be able to fit an entire box in one leg, and you'll no longer spend afternoons hunched over the toy box trying to locate all the logs for your little one's cabin!

219. Hold your kids' marbles.

Marble games are a great way to get the family together on game night. I remember playing marbles with my grandfather and drinking Shirley Temples while my grandmother made her delicious chicken and popovers. The hardest part of playing marbles is finding all the pieces! Store the marbles in the foot of your old pantyhose and tie a knot at the top so they can't escape.

220. Hold bath toys.

Bath toys take up a lot of space and it's not always possible to have a big bucket crowding the bathroom floor. Cut the leg off of an old pair of pantyhose and tie it to a mounted suction cup on the shower wall so that you'll have a place to keep those toys out of the way but in easy reach.

221. Store costume jewelry.

In the last year, we have accumulated more costume jewelry than I care to mention. My daughter is a little princess and loves to dress the part! Although my daughter likes to wear one pink earring and one purple, it's always nice to keep the set together. Store all of the necklaces, bracelets, rings, and earrings in the foot of your old pantyhose, so your little princess is never without her jewels!

222. Make a car seat toy pouch.

It's a good idea to have a few toys in the car for your child to play with, especially on long trips. Many car seats come with a little pouch to hold race cars, paper and markers or little dolls. If your child's car seat didn't come equipped with a toy pouch, you can easily make one by using the foot of your pantyhose. Sew the foot onto the fabric lining of the seat so it hangs open and is easy for kids to access.

223. Store bath crayons.

Bath crayons are great for any aspiring artist! My daughter loves to draw and can now make masterpieces on the tub and shower walls too. To keep the bath crayons from getting mushy and hard to use, store them in the foot of your pantyhose so they can dry properly after every use. Tie your new crayon pouch to a suction cup on the shower wall.

224. Store Barbie shoes.

Barbie's high heel shoes are always falling off and getting lost. To keep Barbie's shoes together when she's not wearing them, store them in the foot of your old pantyhose and remember to tie a knot at the top so they don't fall out.

225. Store a train set.

When my daughter got a wooden train set from Santa last Christmas, I found that it's hard to store all the pull cars and tracks so they're easy to find. Keep everything together by storing the train cars in one leg of your old pantyhose and all the tracks in another. Cut the legs at the top and tie them closed. Arrange them in the toy cart or keep them in a plastic tote.

226. Store train accessories.

Most wooden train sets come with buildings, trees, bridges, and even people. Store all of your child's train accessories in the leg of your old pantyhose. You might want to store this bundle, along with the train and track bundles, in a plastic tote so that the set stays together and isn't misplaced.

227. Hold pacifiers.

No one likes a dirty pacifier, especially a first time mom! After you boil your baby's pacifiers, put them in the foot of your pantyhose and tie the top.

228. Store doll clothes.

My daughter's baby doll didn't come with clothes, and probably wasn't meant to wear any, but my daughter has found her several outfits at our local craft store. The clothes are meant for teddy bears, but they fit my daughter's doll perfectly. A great way to store doll clothes that you didn't plan on having is in the leg of your old pantyhose. You can then put the bundle in your daughter's closet, in the toy cart or under the doll bed.

229. Store bath fizz balls.

These bath balls are a great way to add a little excitement to your child's ordinary bath routine. The balls come in several different colors and when you drop them in the bath, they fizz, make bubbles and change the color of the water. You'll want to keep them close to the tub, so you can reach them while closely supervising your child, but you don't want to keep them where they might get wet. Remove the bath balls from the original packaging and keep them in the foot of your old pantyhose. Add them to your bath toy bucket next to the tub or tie them to a nearby drawer pull or towel rack.

230. Store sidewalk chalk.

If you buy sidewalk chalk by the bucket, you can keep the chalk dry inside its original container. However, if you buy or have received a few pieces of sidewalk chalk that come in a little package, you should remove them from the package and store them in the foot of your old pantyhose. Otherwise the packaging will disintegrate and make a mess when it gets wet outside. If you store the chalk in pantyhose, it will still get wet, but the pantyhose will dry quickly and the chalk won't make a mess.

231. Store pencils.

Do you have any idea how many pencils we have? Me either. We have sports pencils, personalized pencils, heart and rainbow pencils, and even a Hershey kiss pencil. It seems that we need to buy a pencil everywhere we go! A great way to store all of these pencils is in the leg of your old pantyhose. You can then gently place them in the arts and crafts tote so the tips don't break off.

232. Store game pieces.

Game pieces are always falling out of the boxes. Keep them stored in the foot of your old pantyhose so you don't have to hunt for pieces when it comes time to play.

233. Store markers.

My daughter is quite the artist! We have every kind of crayon, pencil, and marker known to man so keeping them organized is no easy task. I decided long ago that our kid stuff would be contained and organized. That usually means removing things from their original packing so they take up less space. Take your kids' markers out of the box and store them in the leg of your old pantyhose. Keep them in a plastic tote with other arts and crafts supplies.

234. Store building blocks.

As with everything else, the original box is too big to store neatly! In case you haven't figured this out yet, I am a neat freak and every little thing has a place—big, bulky blocks are no exception! Save yourself some space by putting the building blocks in the legs of your old pantyhose. They can then go into the toy cart, playroom or closet.

235. Store ping-pong balls.

I loved playing ping-pong when I was a kid, but finding the balls for a game was not fun. A surefire way to keep the ping-pong balls handy is to store them in the leg of your old pantyhose. You can tie the sack to the side of the ping-pong table so that the balls don't get lost.

236. Make an activity bag for the car.

Kids need to be entertained in the car, even on short trips. It makes for a peaceful ride if your kids have something to do! Tie a pair of pantyhose to the headrest of one of your front seats so the legs hang down into the backseat. Fill the hose with your child's favorite activities, such as race cars, coloring books and crayons or washable markers. If your child has a DVD player in the car, you can also store the DVD's in the leg of your pantyhose.

237. Store hand tools.

If you don't have a toolbox, keep your screwdrivers, wrenches, and other hand tools grouped together in pantyhose pouches and hang the pouches in your garage for easy access when you need them.

238. Use to store feminine products.

Okay ladies, this one is for you. If you are looking for a discreet and convenient way to store pantyliners and tampons in your purse or bag, tie them up in the foot of your colored pantyhose. They'll stay clean and will be less conspicuous when you open your purse to take out money.

Chapter 5.

Your Own Backyard

There are hundreds of ways to beautify and improve your yard, starting with the garden. Pantyhose can make great ties for peonies and other top-heavy flowers. They can also be used as suet socks to help attract some beautiful, feathered friends. Or how about a garden party? Decorate your front or backyard with paper lanterns or magical fairies and hang them with thin strips of pantyhose.

239. *Cover tomatoes to keep animals from eating them.*
     All wild animals are looking for nourishment, and it's up to you to decide if they're going to find it at your house! If you want the woodland creatures to leave the tomatoes for you, cover the vines with a pair of old pantyhose.

240. Tie tomato vines to stakes.

Tomato plants need to be staked once they grow tall enough so the tomatoes won't weigh down the vines and end up in the mud. Cut a pair of old pantyhose into long strips and use them to tie the tomato vines to the stakes. The soft material will hold the stems securely without damaging them.

241. Hang squirrel treats.

Squirrels love stealing birdseed from the birds, but they might be distracted if you gave them a little food of their own. Many stores sell a special blend of seed and suet that actually attracts squirrels so that they'll leave the seed for the birds. Cut a strip from the leg of your old pantyhose, tie the squirrel food to a tree branch, and watch them go! Your backyard birds will be truly grateful.

242. Hang a decorative swing.

Obviously, this tip is not suitable for a real swing that will support a child! If you have a tall tree in your garden isle, hanging a little swing from it adds a touch of romance and innocence. Our neighbors have a little pink swing with yellow polka-dots hanging from one of their trees and it looks adorable. You can use the legs from a white pair of pantyhose to suspend the swing and then adorn the knotted ends with leaves or faux flowers.

243. Tie up a garden hose.

Coiling a hose is the easy part, keeping it coiled is not so easy! Once you coil your garden hose, tightly tie the leg of your pantyhose around it to keep it from coming loose. This will not only make retrieving your hose easier, but it will prevent your hose from getting those nasty kinks.

244. Tie roses to a trellis.

Rosebushes need a lot of care in order to flourish. Tying rose canes to a trellis not only provides a nice backdrop, but also provides the roses with the support they need to grow. Cut a pair of old pantyhose into strips and use them to tie the roses to the trellis. You can use white hose for a white trellis and neutral hose for a natural wooden trellis.

245. Protect plants in the winter.

As hard as it is to protect summer plants, protecting plants in the winter presents a whole new set of challenges. The main challenge is to keep plows from dumping all the snow from the street on your shrubs! Put stakes in the ground across the front of your property and stretch pantyhose from stake to stake to make a barrier. Tie the hose tightly. This will work as a visual indicator of your property and will hopefully prevent the plows from crushing your arborvitaes, azaleas, rhododendrons, et cetera.

246. Patch a porch screen.

How is it that insects, with their tiny brains, always manage to find that one little hole in the porch screen? To stop insects from invading your bug-free sanctuary, cut a patch out of your old grey or black pantyhose and use a needle and thread to weave it into the surrounding screen.

247. Make a windsock.

Windsocks are a reliable way to keep tabs on the wind. You can make one out of pantyhose by cutting off the feet and tying the rest of the hose to a pole so it blows in the wind. For an extra creative touch, consider applying seashells or painting stripes on your hose before hanging it outside for everyone's enjoyment.

248. Bunch fresh flowers.

If your idea of flower arranging does not include arranging them stem by stem, simply tie them together with a strip of pantyhose before presenting them to a loved one or situating in a vase. You may want to throw a few marbles in the bottom of your vase to keep them from toppling over.

249. Cover annuals.

A great way to keep bunnies, and other wildlife, off of your flowers and plants is to cover them in the evening with your old pantyhose. It's a damage-free protection for your plants.

250. Decorate for a garden party.

Give your garden a sensational look by hanging fairies in your trees and above your rose bushes. Simply cut a strip from an old pair of pantyhose and use it to suspend your magical garden decorations.

251. Tie peonies.

I love peonies, but they collapse after the first hard rain. Use regular wooden or metal stakes to support your peonies by tying the stalks to the stakes with pantyhose strips. If your peonies are in front of your deck, like mine are, tie the beautiful blooms to your railings with neutral colored hose.

252. Suspend a hanging plant.

I have purchased many plastic pots with hangers attached for my summer plants. Unfortunately, I haven't found one that lasts more than a season. When your hangers break, use a strip of old hose to hang those beautiful impatiens or petunias.

253. Hang a hummingbird feeder.

My parents have a hummingbird feeder with four outlets for the sugar water. It is so nice to see the tiny birds flying in for some refreshment. You can hang the feeder with the leg of your old pantyhose, but tie it tightly to the tree branch so that it is secure.

254. Arrange fresh flowers.

Whether you're hosting a small garden party or an extravagant wedding, flowers are a great way to brighten up a lunch or dinner table. In order to position them just how you want them, they need to be tightly secured. If you don't own a green sponge block, like those at the florist, stretch a swatch of old hose across the top of your vase and secure it there with clear tape. Push the stems through, one at a time, to create a masterpiece. Let some leaves and flowers hang down to disguise the pantyhose rim.

255. Wrap plants.

If you're transplanting a little tree or plant from one part of your yard to another, it's important to keep the roots in tact until you're ready to complete the job. Tree nurseries use burlap. If you don't have any burlap handy, why not wrap the roots in pantyhose instead? Use the seat of the pantyhose and tie the seat securely to the plant itself using the legs.

256. Mark the deep end of a pool.

Don't take any chances! Little kids may not understand the concept of a deep end so make sure it's well marked. Fill the legs of your old pantyhose with small blocks of Styrofoam and attach several legs together to float them across the pool where you want them to beware.

257. Hang outdoor lanterns.

Little paper lanterns look so pretty hanging from tree branches at an evening party. Use pantyhose strips to suspend the lanterns for your next gathering. Your garden will look so inviting and enchanting!

258. Cover a watering can spout.

It's hard to control the water flow from a watering can. Too much water at once could drown delicate flowers and little plants. If your watering can has a big cover or if it doesn't have one at all, stretch the foot of your old hose over the spout to control the water flow.

259. Display place cards.

If you're having a big party and don't have the room to display 100 place cards on a table, try this: Staple the legs of your white pantyhose to the top of a giant topiary and attach the place cards (in alphabetical order) to the pantyhose legs. The guests will be able to find their place cards easily because they will be at eye level. Place the topiary at the entrance to your garden or tent so that guests know where to go once they get inside the party.

260. Hang balloons for a party.

Carry your party theme outside and hang color coordinated balloons on your deck or patio with old pantyhose strips.

261. Decorate a topiary.

Topiaries make a beautiful accent to any table and are great for any season. I like to put one on my mantle at Christmas time with a pretty piece of ribbon or tulle tied around the pole for added sparkle. Instead of ribbon, use white pantyhose to decorate topiaries that will grace a dinner table or neutral toned hose to make a woodland effect for a garden party.

262. Tie on a corsage.

Every girl deserves a corsage once in a while! Cut a few stems from your garden to make a corsage and use a strip of pantyhose to tie it around your wrist. What better way to flaunt your gardening skills than to wear the fruits of your labor!

263. Store bulbs.

We have mice in our shed and they ate their way through two bags of tulip bulbs last year. If your bag of bulbs is torn, ripped, or chewed apart by mice, remove the bulbs and store them in a leg of your old pantyhose. Move them to a mouse-free location.

264. Tie your gardening tools together.

Tie your rakes, hoes and shovels together with pantyhose legs before you put them in a moving vehicle. This will keep them from rolling round and causing damage to your vehicle or falling off the back of your truck.

265. Mark the gas and oil cans.

While it's easy to get them confused, it's important to keep lawnmower gas separate from weed whacker oil. Tie the leg of your old pantyhose to the weed whacker can and tie the same color pantyhose to the actual weed whacker so you know which can holds which fluid.

266. Cover outdoor drains to keep the leaves out.

Clogged outdoor drains can redirect water into your basement. To keep your house dry and your drain free of leaves and debris, stretch a section of pantyhose over the top of the drain.

267. Safely cut a tree branch.

Tree work can be dangerous and requires some safety measures to be taken. Before you cut off a tree branch, tie the branch to the tree with a pair of old pantyhose so that it doesn't snap back at you when you start to cut. Once you've made the cut, remove the hose and let the branch fall.

268. Store seeds.

Seed packets usually go on sale at the end of the season, so it's a great time to stock up. Once you have purchased your seed packets for next year's blooms, store them in the foot of your old pantyhose and store them near your gardening supplies until you're ready to plant them.

269. Store plant pots.

Stack your pots inside of one another and then put them into the leg of your old pantyhose. Be sure to tie a knot at the top to keep unwanted guests, like bugs and mice, from making their home there!

270. Block weeds from growing.

This may take a while, but it will save you plenty of time in the summer when you have to weed! Lay several pairs of pantyhose over the dirt surface of your garden. Cover the entire surface if possible. Cut holes in the pantyhose where you will plant your flowers. Plant your annuals and cover the entire garden with a thick layer of mulch. The nylon material should stop weeds from growing and overtaking your garden.

271. Protect yourself from splinters

It's easy to get splinters when you're using garden tools with wooden handles. Cut the legs from a pair of pantyhose and wrap one around each hand so you're protected as you work.

272. Make a "sock feeder" for the birds.

Cut the legs from your old pantyhose and stuff them with a delicious blend of peanut butter and seed. Make several sock feeders and hang them all outside for your feathered friends.

273. Fill with thistle to feed finches.

Not all birds enjoy the same type of seed, so make sure you're hanging the right type of seed for the birds that flock to your yard. Finches enjoy thistle seed (also called Niger), and you can easily make a feeder out of an old pantyhose leg. Simply fill the foot with thistle seed, tie it at the top, and hang on a tree branch.

274. Hang a bird feeder.

Our bird feeder is always getting knocked on the ground by squirrels or by the wind. Unfortunately, feeders aren't always made with a strong hanger that can withstand the weight of a small animal! If you're tired of trying to repair your feeder and tired of your lawn being "seeded," try hanging your feeder with the leg of your old pantyhose. Make sure you tie a tight knot so that it doesn't come undone.

275. Hang a birdseed bell.

Seed bells are so light, they can easily be blown off a tree limb if they're not hung securely. Cut the leg from an old pair of pantyhose and use it to hang your seed bell. After tying the hose to the bell, wrap the remainder around the limb before tying it to the tree. It will be very hard for the wind or a creature to knock it down if it's wrapped securely around the tree.

276. Tie the top of your birdfeeder closed.

We have done everything to try and provide our birds with seed, short of hand feeding them. The problem is we have a family of squirrels that swings from the feeder until the top comes off and the whole contraption falls to the ground. Once the seed is on the ground, the squirrels eat to their heart's content. To maintain a bird-friendly feeder, tie the top of it closed with a strip of old pantyhose.

PART 2.

Creative Notions

PART 2.

Creative Notions

Chapter 6

Just for Kids

Kids love crafts! Pick a neat project to do each week using a pair of old pantyhose. You'll be surprised at how fast you go through them—and, as a special bonus, your kids will think you're a genius! Pantyhose are also perfect for keeping all those tiny toy pieces tidy and together.

277. Store little toy balls.

Our house is filled with small balls from various toys, and we can never find the right ball for the right toy at the right time! A great way to store small balls is in the leg of an old pair of pantyhose.

278. Make a Halloween spider costume.

At some point, every child has his or her heart set on a particular costume for Halloween. This year, my daughter wanted to be a Hoodsie Cup! Inevitably, the year that your child wants to be a spider is the year that the costume designers create a dragonfly costume instead. Have no fear, Mommy is here . . . with her old black pantyhose and some stuffing! Cut the legs off three pairs of black pantyhose and fill the six legs with stuffing. Make sure that you really stuff them so that they'll stand out. Once the legs are stuffed, tie them to a black belt so that there are three on each side. Dress your child in a black leotard and tights, put the belt around her waist, and add some cobwebs for a spooky effect! Halloween made easy!

279. Make a dachshund toy.

Every child loves to have a stuffed dog to walk on a leash, feed pretend food to, and sleep with at night. It's better to have a soft animal for your child, especially if it'll be snuggled in bed with them. Cut the leg off of a brown pair of pantyhose and stuff it in order to form the body. You can stuff the feet of your pantyhose and use them for a head, ears, feet and tail. Once those individual feet are stuffed, simply sew them onto the body with brown thread. Add buttons for eyes and a nose and sew a red line for the mouth.

280. Stuff teddy bears to give as gifts.

The introduction for this book says it all! Who doesn't love a teddy bear? You can use any type of material for the fur—fabric stores have floral, gingham, plush fur and quilted varieties to choose from. Make your outline, sew roughly halfway around, and stuff with pantyhose to fill the head, body, arms, and legs. Close up the bear, and sew on some cute buttons for the eyes and nose. Sew a little line for the mouth. Who knows, your child may be able to pass down their "Teddy Reddy" to children of their own someday!

281. Make rag dolls for little girls.

Do you remember Raggedy Ann and Andy? They were great dolls that could go everywhere and then be thrown into the washing machine for a much-needed bath. Today, many dolls can only be hand-washed or spot-cleaned and are difficult to keep clean. If you're looking for a doll that can accompany your child on errands and to play dates and then be thoroughly cleaned, look no further. You can easily make a rag doll with cotton fabric and stuff it with your old pantyhose.

282. Make Hershey's Kisses party favors.

I've received and prepared many party favors, and I've learned that it's not the expensive and well-thought-out gifts that the kids are excited about, it's the chocolate! Hershey's Kisses are great, because they're small enough for the kids to eat in one bite and they don't make a huge mess. Cut the foot off of your old pantyhose, fill with several Kisses, and tie with a pretty ribbon. White pantyhose are great for spring and summer parties, and you can always adorn them with a little flower or butterfly in addition to the ribbon.

283. Bandage a stuffed animal.

Kids love to take care of their make-believe pets. When a favorite stuffed animal gets a boo boo, show your child how to make an animal bandage out of nude pantyhose.

284. Make a Spiderman mask.

Spiderman is still all the rage, and kids everywhere are watching Spiderman movies and playing dress-up at home! If you cut the foot off of an old pair of pantyhose, you can stretch it over a ball and paint it to look like Spiderman. That way, the facial features will be in the right places when the ball is removed and your child puts the mask over his head.

285. Make and decorate sock puppets.

Kids love to express themselves, and puppet theater is a great way to do it. Use a cardboard box for the stage, and have your children decorate the feet of your old hose any way they like to make puppets.

286. Make a set of juggling balls.

Pantyhose make great juggling balls because they're soft and safe to play with in the house. Simply cut the feet off of your old pantyhose, stuff them with the rest of the hose, and either sew or tie them closed.

287. Make a bowling ball and pins.

Taking a toddler bowling for the first time can eat up an entire day. Although it's fun for them, it's very tiring for you! Make a set at home to practice with, so that everyone is able to play the next time you go to a bowling alley. To make the pins, cut the legs off of your pantyhose, put a lightweight coaster in the bottom of the foot, and stuff with the rest of the hose so that it's packed tightly. The pins should be able to stand up on their own. To make the bowling ball, cut the foot off of your pantyhose, stuff with the remaining hose so that it's firm and sew the top closed. Get ready, roll, and strike!

288. Skim the kiddie pool.

I love getting out the kiddie pool for play dates and birthday parties because it's a great way to keep kids outside and cool. Most people fill the pool an hour or so before the kids get in so that the water has time to warm up in the sun. Of course, if you leave the pool out like this, leaves and bugs will find their way in. Use your old pantyhose to skim the pool and get it clean before the kids hop in.

289. Make a slingshot.

Okay, I know slingshots are dangerous but every kid wants one. Find a stick that makes a "V" at the top and tie a strip of pantyhose between the prongs. Restrict your kids to using soft projectiles like hacky sacks and monitor them closely as they send them soaring through the air.

290. Make a weight for a small boat.

My young niece and nephew live near the ocean and spend their summers at sailing camp. When they're not sailing Optis, they're down at the beach playing with toy boats. Obviously, you would not want to rely on a pantyhose weight to secure a real boat, but it's perfect for a toy boat. Fill the foot or leg of your old pantyhose with small rocks and tie to your toddler's toy boat so that it doesn't float away when they're not looking.

291. Make replacement shoelaces.

Unfortunately, shoelaces don't always last as long as shoes! Once the laces are thin and frayed, it only takes one strong pull to rip them right in half. When your child's shoelaces become worn, replace them with long strips of pantyhose (tie two together if necessary). Use a sewing needle to lace them through the holes.

292. Carry schoolbooks.

To make it easier for your kids to carry their books to school or the library, stack the books on top of each other with the largest ones on the bottom and tie a leg of pantyhose around the length and width of the stack to make a little package. Tie a firm knot at the top so your child has something to grab onto.

293. Fill with coins to give out at Halloween.

Many kids collect for UNICEF at Halloween when they go trick-or-treating. Put some coins in the foot of your old pantyhose and tie with orange and black ribbon. When the kids come to your door, you won't have to dig through your purse or fiddle with a collection box—just drop a coin pouch in each bag.

294. Make Christmas candy bundles.

Fill the foot of your clean pantyhose with chocolate coins or chocolate Santas and tie with a pretty red and green ribbon. These bundles can be put into stockings or placed in a candy dish on your coffee table.

295. Make goodie bags for a Hanukkah party.

If you celebrate Hanukkah, or have friends that do, this is a great way to make a little something for party guests. Wrap chocolate dreidels in the foot of your clean white pantyhose and tie with a royal blue ribbon.

296. Make Easter candy bundles.

My mother, I mean the Easter Bunny, used to fill my Easter basket with several bundles of candy. She used to put eggs, M&M's, jelly beans, and Hershey Kisses in her old pantyhose eggs. You remember the plastic eggs that L'eggs used to come in? They were great for Easter baskets! I don't think pantyhose are sold in eggs anymore, so try this instead: Put wrapped candies in the foot of your clean pantyhose and tie with pastel ribbon. The candy bundles will take up less space than the plastic eggs, so you can really fill that basket up. What kid won't love that?

297. Tie pinwheels to your child's stroller.

All kids love pinwheels, but few can blow hard enough to really spin them. Tie your toddler's pinwheel to the front of his or her stroller with a strip of old pantyhose. Position the pinwheel so it spins as you push. Your child will be speechless!

298. Tie a flag to your antenna.

For some reason, people like to decorate their cars. For me, decorating my car would be like painting my cat's nails— why bother? But, for those of you who enjoy putting ornaments on your vehicles, use strips of pantyhose to mount a flag to your antenna and proudly it may wave.

299. Tie a flag to your child's stroller or wagon.

The next town over holds a HUGE 4th of July parade and celebration every year. Every house on our street is decorated to the nines and people go all out with red, white, and blue. When we hike to the parade with my daughter in tow in her decorated wagon, she feels like she's part of the parade and, in a sense, she is. Next July, tie two American flags to the back of your child's stroller or wagon with strips of pantyhose and proudly march to your neighborhood parade.

300. Plug your ears.

If the neighbors are keeping you up at night and you can't find a pair of ear plugs, make your own with an old pair of pantyhose. Scrunch up a small piece of pantyhose material and place it in your ear to help muffle the sounds and get back to sleep.

301. Make maracas.

My daughter has loved playing the maracas ever since we brought her to Gymboree music class at age one. Music toys are great for kids but they're over priced and some of them, like the maracas, can easily be made at home. Fill the feet of your old pantyhose with beans and tie a knot at the top to make soft maracas.

302. Make no-scratch mittens for an infant.

Infants seem to have long fingernails, partly because all the milk and formula they drink makes their nails grow faster and partly because every new parent hates to cut a baby's tiny fingernails. When these nails get long, or have sharp edges, infants tend to scratch themselves when they rub their eyes. Cover your infant's hands with soft mittens made from the feet of your pantyhose to prevent accidental scratches. Sew some elastic in the top so they gather at the wrist and stay on your child's hands.

303. Make a doll hammock.

Why shouldn't your child's baby have all the comforts of home? Find a pretty piece of fabric, cut it into a rectangle and sew four pantyhose strips (one for each corner) to the fabric. Now tie the four loose ends to the legs of two kitchen chairs and give the doll the afternoon off.

304. Make a seatbelt for a doll.

My daughter's baby has her own car seat and yes, it is buckled into our car at all times. Unfortunately, the doll's car seat did not come with a five-point harness, so we had to make do. You can use the leg from an old pair of pantyhose to strap your child's baby doll into her seat to keep her safe. I think that telling you not to do this for a REAL child goes without saying!

305. Make pants for a large doll.

Have you seen the life-sized Barbie doll? Unfortunately, the toy store doesn't sell clothes for this doll and we all know that Barbies need a fashion wardrobe! To make pants for your child's larger dolls, cut the feet off of your old pantyhose and sew elastics at the bottom of the legs for a custom fit. Use different colored pantyhose to expand the doll's wardrobe and apply beads, glitter or flowers for a little pizazz. Now, that's high fashion!

306. Make tights for a large doll.

If you're going to make a nice skirt for the big Barbie, she will need a nice pair of tights . . . especially if her skirt will be short!

307. Use to make a mobile.

Attach interesting little toys, paper cut-outs or drawings to a wire hanger using pantyhose strips of varying lengths. Hang it in your child's room so they can take pride in their special creation.

308. Make a basketball net.

Basketball nets don't last forever, so think about using your old pantyhose to make your next swoosh! If your current net is torn or in bad shape, remove it from the rim and sew on the seat of your old hose instead. Simply cut the seat wide open so that the basketballs can fit right through.

309. Hang baby shoes.

Baby shoes are great reminders of when your children were little. My sister actually used her husband's baby shoes to decorate her son's nursery. If the laces are worn, hang them on the wall using thin strips of pantyhose. To add an extra special touch to your hanging baby shoes, tie a pretty bow at the top to draw more attention to the display.

310. Make a scarf for a snowman.

We waited weeks for the right kind of packing snow this past winter. Once it arrived, we made snowmen, snow penguins and snow Christmas trees! I hate to leave one of our nice scarves outside on a snowman. If you're like me, you'd rather use it to keep your family warm than wrap it around a pile of dirty ice. Here's an easy way to spare your winter scarves: Cut the leg from an old pair of pantyhose and wrap it around your snowman's neck to make a scarf. Be sure to use black or navy hose so that it stands out to onlookers!

311. Make a doggy costume.

Pantyhose can make great dog ears for your kid's costume. Simply stuff the seat of your pantyhose under a hat and let the legs hang down on either side of your child's head like dog ears.

312. Make a backpack handle.

It seems to me that kids are sent home with more and more, homework each year! Carrying all those books can be a real burden, especially on your child's back. Sew a section of leg from your pantyhose to the top of your child's backpack so that he or she has the option of carrying those heavy books by hand.

313. Secure rattles to a stroller.

My daughter loved Curious George when she was a baby. She had a Curious George rattle with a plastic ring that we tied to the side of her stroller. She could snuggle "Stroller George" if she wanted to or she could throw him outside the stroller and he'd hang until she pulled him back in. Either way, we knew that her favorite monkey was safe and wouldn't be lost. Use the leg from an old pair of pantyhose to secure your child's favorite rattle to the side of the stroller. Your baby will be entertained and you won't need to worry about picking up dropped toys along your merry way.

314. Make a bug net for a stroller.

I hate bugs and I certainly don't like them bothering my baby. It's important to protect your children, especially if they are infants, from mosquitoes because you never know if they are diseased or not. Stretch a pair of pantyhose over the front of your child's stroller and attach it there to help keep unwanted bugs at bay.

315. Hold sunglasses and sunscreen for a pool party favor.

This is a favor that you can hand out to your guests when they arrive. If they came prepared, they can take the sunglasses and sunscreen home with them and if they didn't come prepared, they will have what they need.

316. Hold flip-flops for a summer party favor.

Summer birthdays are the best! Not only are the parties easier because of weather and a vast array of party themes, but the favors are easier to put together too. My older sister gave me this idea for my daughter's birthday party: Buy some cute flip-flops for each partygoer, put them in a leg of white pantyhose and tie with a pretty, summer-striped ribbon.

317. Make a sunhat strap.

Many sunhats for children over one year old don't come with chin straps. Since kids are apt to pull off their sunhat as soon as they feel too hot, you need a way to keep that hat on their head so they stay protected from those harmful rays. Cut two strips of pantyhose, sew one to either side of your child's sunhat and tie the two ends together in a cute little bow under your child's chin.

318. Make reins for a rocking horse.

"Go, Funnyside!" That's what my daughter yelled as she rode her plush rocking horse while watching the Kentucky Derby a few years ago. If your child's horse doesn't have reins, use the legs of your pantyhose to make some. Wrap the hose underneath the horse's neck and cross it around his nose like a muzzle, leaving the remaining hose for your child to hold onto while riding.

319. Decorate your child's rocking horse.

If your child's horse wins the Triple Crown, braid several colored pantyhose strips into his mane and tail so that he looks like a winner on his victory walk!

320. String beads for a bracelet.

It doesn't take long for a girl to learn about, and want, baubles! If you have some big beads, string them on a strip of pantyhose to make a bracelet for your little one.

321. Make a guitar strap.

Not if you're going out on tour, of course! My daughter has a real guitar, but it didn't come with a strap. You can make a strap for your child's guitar by tying a leg of pantyhose to the guitar base and attaching the other end to the top.

322. Make a necktie for a cowboy hat.

My daughter loves country music, specifically Shania Twain. For her birthday this year, my father gave her a cowgirl hat with matching pink leather cowgirl boots. She was beside herself! Unfortunately, cowboy hats don't come with a strap and often fall off while your child is line dancing or riding a bucking bronco. Use a hot glue gun to attach two pantyhose strips, one for each side, on the inside rim so that the hat stays put.

323. Make a holster for a cowboy costume.

If your cowboy's squirt gun needs a holster, make one out of an old pair of pantyhose. Shorten one of the legs by tying a knot just a few inches from the top and cutting off the remainder. Now cut an opening at the top of that leg so the gun can fit through. Tie the other leg around their waist like a belt and attach it to the seat of the hose. Have them meet you in the backyard at "high noon."

324. Secure bicycles to a bike rack.

Have kids, will travel! If you're planning a summer getaway, don't forget the bikes. Once you've loaded your bikes onto the rack, tie them tightly with the legs of your old pantyhose.

325. Make a backpack for a doll.

I don't know about your daughter's baby doll, but mine needs to have just about everything that my daughter has. Mothering starts so early! If you have a small purse lying around, you can easily make it into a little backpack for a doll. Simply cut two short pantyhose strips and sew them onto either side of the purse. Now place the purse on the doll's back and tie the two strips around the doll's arms.

326. Secure a basket to a bicycle.

A young girl's bicycle needs everything from a basket to shining streamers. If your daughter's bicycle didn't come with a little basket, you can tie one onto the front of her bike with the leg of your old pantyhose. The pantyhose are thick enough to hold it in place and will dry quickly if left out in the rain.

327. Extend overall straps.

We've all been there. The money is a little tight and your children's clothes are a little short. Kids grow at such a fast pace that it's hard to keep up with their wardrobe necessities. I have found that certain clothing items, like overalls, don't last as long as regular pants because of the straps. You can lengthen the overall straps by tying strips of pantyhose to the ends and then tying them around the button on the bib. I don't suggest sending your kids to school this way, but it certainly works well for play clothes.

328. Make a pretend veil.

Every little girl fantasizes about marrying Prince Charming, and every princess needs a veil! Cut open just the leg of a pair of white or off-white pantyhose. Round out the bottom edge with scissors and attach it to a plastic headband with super glue. Here comes the bride!

329. Make a pouch for a pencil sharpener.

Why is that a child's pencil sharpener doesn't come fitted with a cover to catch the shavings? To keep the shavings from falling out all over your floor, attach the foot of your pantyhose to the end of the sharpener that dispenses shavings. Use a glue gun to secure it all the way around.

330. Make a fairy skirt.

My daughter's friend loves Tinkerbell and loves to play dress up. Buying a character dress-up outfit at the mall can be pricey, so spend a little time at home to get the same effect. Snip the feet off of a pair of pantyhose and cut the legs open lengthwise. Cut slits into one of the long edges and wrap your design around your child's waist with the slits hanging down. Sprinkle a little fairy dust and she's ready to fly!

331. Make leaves for a fall picture.

Kids can make wonderful fall pictures by gluing real fallen leaves to construction paper. If your kids want to get crafty and there aren't any good leaves around, try cutting leaf shapes out of your neutral, tan or brown pantyhose. Your kids can glue them to the paper and you can hang it on the fridge and make them proud.

332. Make pom-poms.

My two older sisters used to parade me around the soccer field when they were cheerleaders. I loved the attention, but didn't like the fact that they didn't have kid-sized pom-poms for me to shake. Since then, I have found a great way to make smaller pom-poms for little cheerleaders. If you go to a home improvement store, such as Home Depot, you can get plastic handles for lugging paint cans around the store. Cut your old pantyhose into several strips and attach them to the plastic handles until they're nice and full. Your little ones will love to shake them and the plastic handles are great for little hands!

333. Secure teethers to a car seat.

I know how hard it is to drive safely and tend to an unhappy baby in the back seat. This can be especially difficult when driving with infants who need their teether, because an infant car seat faces backwards. Make your life easier and the roads safer by tying your baby's teething rings to their car seat with a strip of pantyhose. If your child isn't old enough to grab it himself, you can at least find it more easily. Please make sure that the pantyhose strip is short so that it's not a choking hazard!

334. Tie a pacifier to a diaper bag.

If dirt doesn't bother you, then tie a pacifier to your baby's diaper bag. It won't be the cleanest pacifier around, but it will be there when you need it. Cut a strip from your pantyhose and tie one end to the pacifier loop and the other end to the diaper bag strap or an inside loop.

335. Make a piñata for a party.

When you choose to have a piñata at your child's party, you leave yourself wide open to kids fighting, pushing, and accidentally slugging each other with a bat! Corporate America has wisely begun to offer piñatas that drop candy when you pull a ribbon so kids no longer need to beat it to the ground. If your local party store doesn't have a pull down piñata to go with your party theme, get out your scissors and make one. Cut the leg from an old pair of pantyhose, tie up the open end, and cut a slit at the top to use as a candy flap. Tie a brightly colored ribbon to that flap and lightly stitch the piñata closed after you fill it up with goodies. Tie other colored ribbons around the flap so that each party guest can take a turn. Decorate the outside of the piñata any way that you like. For example, you can attach princess decorations for a princess party or Matchbox cars for a racing party.

336. Make a changing pad.

A lot of people choose to use a dresser top to change their babies instead of buying an expensive changing table that they will be done with in three years. If you choose to use a dresser top as a changing table, you'll need to buy or make a changing pad so that your baby has some support. If you choose to make one, try wrapping a foam pad in your old pantyhose. The pantyhose are soft and can be glued or tied around the bottom of the pad.

337. Carry crayons.

I always have an ample supply of crayons in my purse for restaurants, meetings, and car rides. I don't know about your purse, but mine is stuffed to the gills! Crayon boxes take up a lot of room and are awkward to store in the side of your purse. If you want to save space, remove the crayons from the cardboard box and store in the foot of your old pantyhose.

338. Make Halloween goody bags.

Kids expect to get candy for Halloween and parties are no exception! You can easily make goody bags for your next spook fest by cutting the legs off of your black pantyhose, filling them with chocolate eyeballs, gummy worms, and candy corn, and then tying them closed with a bright orange ribbon. Boo!

339. Wash a baby doll.

You need to use extra care when putting your baby's baby in the washing machine so that the doll doesn't get ripped. We put my daughter's baby in a net so that she is contained and can't get caught on anything. The leg of your old pantyhose will make a great net to protect your little one's lovey.

340. Make a hopscotch marker.

Kids of all ages love to play hopscotch. Unfortunately, the hopscotch games at the store don't come with a heavy marker. For example, my daughter's princess hopscotch game came with little plastic hearts that don't stay where they land, so it's hard to stick to the rules. Make sure that your kids are playing a fair game by providing them with a heavy marker that will stay put when it lands. Fill the foot of your pantyhose with some rocks and tie a knot tightly at the top. Happy hopping!

341. Make doll socks.

I know this may sound ridiculous, but little girls can be very mothering and will want their babies to have everything that they have. For larger dolls, cut the feet off of your old pantyhose and sew elastics around the top of each foot. For smaller dolls, trim the feet a little before sewing the elastics around the top.

342. Make Easter grass.

Easter grass can be harmful to pets and especially young
children because it poses a severe choking hazard. If you
want to play it safe this Easter, cut your old pantyhose into
strips and line the bottom of your child's Easter basket with
the soft nylon.

343. Make Easter chicks.

This is easier than it sounds! First draw an outline of a
chick onto a pair of white pantyhose, cut two shapes out
and sew about halfway around. You can then stuff the chick
with old pantyhose strips and then stitch up the remaining
fabric. Once the chick is stuffed, add the eyes and a beak.
You can even glue a feather on as the tail.

344. Wrap a bar of soap.

It's smart to form good habits early. Encourage your kids to
wash themselves in the tub by wrapping a bar of soap in easy-
to-grip fabric. This way it won't slip all over the place when
they try to hold it. It's easy to make your soap kid-friendly by
wrapping a bar in the foot of your old pantyhose. Remember
to tie a knot at the top so the soap doesn't fall out!

345. Make a hacky sack ball.

These were very popular when I was growing up and they're still popular with today's kids. Cut the foot off of your pantyhose, stuff the rest of the pantyhose inside the foot and stitch it closed for a sack you can truly hack.

346. Make a mummy costume.

Halloween is always right around the corner, at least according to the mass marketers! Make your child an original costume this year out of your old pantyhose. You can make a great mummy costume by wrapping your child in the legs of your old white pantyhose. Don't forget to leave holes for the eyes, nose, and mouth!

347. Make candy bundles for a piñata.

Kids love to knock the candy out of a piñata, but parents don't like finding chocolate in the lawn mower. Keep the piñata, but make it neater! Use the feet of your old pantyhose to hold several pieces of candy and tie with a ribbon at the top. Make enough candy bundles so that each child gets the same amount and put them inside the piñata. Your kids will be happy and your lawn will be neat!

348. Make balloon strings for a party.

If you blow up your balloons at home, your kids will need something to hold them with. Instead of using curling ribbon, which pets can choke on, cut your pantyhose into thin strips and tie to the balloons.

349. Make a jester's hat.

This requires a bit of imagination! Put the pantyhose seat on your child's head so that the legs hang down by their ears. Cut the legs short and tie them at the ends. Consider attaching some colorful felt and jingle bells to make it pop!

350. Tie a doll to your child's bicycle.

My daughter hates to be without her baby doll but loves to ride her bike, so we joined them together. Secure a doll to the back of your child's bike with a leg of pantyhose. Wrap it tightly and knot securely. Your child will be happy and her baby will be safe.

351. Make a doll pillow.

Dolls are people too . . . at least in our house! To make a pillow for your child's doll, cut two fabric rectangles, sew halfway around, stuff with your old pantyhose and stitch up. Your child's baby will rest easy tonight!

352. Make sheets for a doll bed.

Cut open the legs of your old pantyhose lengthwise to make wide strips and use them as sheets for a doll bed. Cut some fabric of equal size for a doll blanket and you have a complete doll bedding set.

353. Make a child's travel pillow.

What kid doesn't sleep in the car? I remember taking road trips with my parents and younger sister and there was barely room for all of our gear, never mind two full sized pillows. You can easily make a small travel pillow for your child by sewing two pieces of fabric together and filling with old pantyhose. Pick a nice, soft fabric like flannel or fleece so it's extra comfy!

354. Make a pillowcase.

You can stretch the leg of your pantyhose over your child's toddler sized pillow to make a pillowcase. This is a great temporary solution when you're traveling or when all your other pillowcases are in the wash.

355. Line a hamper.

Children's hampers are small enough to line with a pair of old pantyhose. No need to buy a heavy canvas liner if you're using a laundry basket to transport clothes from your child's bedroom to the laundry room.

356. Make a hat flap for sun protection.

Most parents are pretty careful about protecting their child's heads from the sun, but often forget about the backs of their necks. It might not be necessary for girls with long hair, but little boys with short hair should have a hat with flaps in the back to block the sun's harmful rays. To make a sunhat for your child, layer large sections of pantyhose and sew them to the back of your child's summer hat, making sure that the material hangs low enough to cover the back of their neck.

357. Carry Rollerblades.

Kids often tie their Rollerblade laces together and swing them over their shoulders to carry them home. Bigger, heavier Rollerblades need a stronger handle in case the laces break. Tie a strip of pantyhose between the two Rollerblades and wear the blades over your shoulder to help support the load.

358. Hang a strobe light.

Teenagers love to dance. You can turn your teenager's bedroom into a club by using dark wall paint and hanging a strobe light from the ceiling. Use a strip of old black pantyhose to suspend the light. Add some glitter to the hose for a more dramatic effect.

359. Make a beach bag.

The leg of your old pantyhose is great for storing shovels, sunscreen, arm bubbles, and more!

360. Make a Halloween skeleton.

Halloween-lovers put a lot of extra effort into celebrating this creepy holiday. If you're one of those people, try making a skeleton out of your old white pantyhose. First, cut off the legs and lay them flat on a table. Draw bones on them with black marker and stuff them with other pairs of white pantyhose. Use the longest "bone" in the center and tie the others onto it for arms and legs. Cut another leg in half and draw a skeleton face on it. Fill it until it's big and round like a head and tie the skeleton body to the bottom. Once the skeleton is formed, hang it from a tree to spook your trick-or-treaters.

361. Make ghosts.

Stuff the seat of your white pantyhose and tie it closed at the waist. The knot would be the top of the ghost's head. Paint a scary expression on your ghost's face. Cut slits along the two legs to make them look like spooky arms and hang your ghost from a tree on Halloween. Boo!

362. Decorate for an "under the sea" party.

Ariel is the one princess that my daughter likes! If your daughter loves *The Little Mermaid* and is planning an "under the sea" party, you can use your neutral pantyhose as fish netting. Cut several pairs of pantyhose open, tack to the walls, and apply seashells, seaweed, and sea creatures.

363. Make gloves for rollerblading.

It is important to protect your hands, in case you fall, when you go rollerblading. I look like an accident victim going down the street with my helmet, gloves, and elbow and knee protectors—but at least I'm safe! Cut the feet off of your old pantyhose and sew a nylon or suede piece of fabric into the middle of the foot in order to protect your palms. Cut finger holes along the seam and you're ready to roll!

364. Keep hair back under a bike helmet.

My daughter loves to ride her bike but when her hair falls in her eyes, she tends to let go of the handle bars to push it aside! Falls are inevitable (which is why kids should always wear bike helmets), but this kind of fall can be prevented. Stretch the foot of your old pantyhose over your child's hair to keep it from falling into her eyes. Put the helmet on over the hairnet and she's ready to ride!

365. Store dirty diapers.

If you don't have a Diaper Genie, you can create a similar contraption to control dirty diaper odor. It won't be as easy as using a Genie, but it will certainly clean things up a bit. You can line your diaper pail with any kind of trash bag, but the scented ones will make your baby's nursery smell nicer. Once you've lined the diaper pail, stretch a pair of pantyhose around the rim of the pail. After you've changed your baby, put the dirty diaper in the bottom of a pantyhose leg, twist and tie a knot to keep that smell contained. Repeat this for each dirty diaper and once you've filled up a pair of pantyhose, replace it with another pair.

366. Wrap water balloons.

Every kid loves to play with water balloons in the summertime, but latex poses a serious choking hazard to young children. Let the younger kids in on the fun by placing the filled water balloons in the feet of your old pantyhose and tying a knot at the top. The water balloons will still pop, but the bits of latex will stay contained instead of going all over your lawn.

367. Make bean bags for a bean toss game.

Do you remember the bean toss game from carnivals and fairs? I do and I loved trying to throw the bean bag into the clown's mouth! You can create the same game for your kids to enjoy at home. Construct the board out of a piece of plywood and paint a clown face on it. Make a hole where the mouth would go and lean it against the wall. To make the bean bags, cut the feet off of your old pantyhose, fill them with beans and tie a knot at the top. Let your kids take turns trying to throw the bean bag in the clown's mouth.

368. Make a limbo stick.

It's just as easy for two people to hold the leg of your old pantyhose as it is for them to hold a stick. You can even tie both ends of the pantyhose to two sturdy pieces of furniture so everyone can play!

369. Make a bowtie for a clown costume.

I think clowns are kind of scary, but I know that I am in the minority here. If your child wants to be a clown, you can easily make a bowtie for the costume out of your old pantyhose. Use the leg from any colored hose you'd like and paint polka dots on it using fabric paint. Once the paint has dried, attach it to your child's costume at the neckline and then tie it into a big bow with floppy loops on each side.

370. Decorate flowery flip-flops.

This is a fun project to do with your daughter and her friends. Buy a few pairs of inexpensive plain rubber flip-flops and cut a pair of colored pantyhose into little strips. Glue the pantyhose strips to the center of the thong to make a decorative flower. What a fun summer look!

371. Make a jump rope.

If you have ever had a play date at your house, you know that it's almost impossible to have enough of the same toy for everyone to be satisfied. Because they're less expensive, it is possible to have enough jump ropes for everyone if you don't mind making them yourself. Cut the legs off of your old pantyhose and tie a few of them together until the length is just right for jumping. Tie a loop at each end to use as a handle.

372. Make a ping-pong table net.

For some reason, the nets on our ping-pong table never fared well. It may have been due to the excessive force with which my three brothers played ping-pong, but I'm not pointing any fingers! When your net has been beaten down, cut open the leg of a pair of pantyhose (without the feet) and stretch the long piece of material across your ping-pong table. Attach to both ends with strong tape for a makeshift net.

Chapter 7.

Tricks for Teachers

Most teachers work on a modest salary and oftentimes, their school is short on supplies. For teachers looking for fun ideas and innovative ways to save money on classroom supplies, pantyhose are the perfect answer. They get an A for effort if you ask me.

373. Make a blindfold.

This is primarily for preschool classes. The leg of your old pantyhose makes a great blindfold for a quick game of pin the tail on the donkey.

374. Hang a bathroom pass.

When I was in school, we had to use a "lav pass" to be excused for the bathroom. The lav pass was usually thrown on the teacher's desk. Use a strip of pantyhose to hang the bathroom pass on the wall near the door. Not only will you have more desk space, but the kids can grab it themselves instead of interrupting your class to ask you for it.

375. Hold carrots for a zoo field trip.

My daughter's preschool takes little field trips to the zoo across the street. All of the kids love to feed carrots to the donkeys and llamas, but not every mother remembers to bring them along. Throw a few carrots into the foot of your old pantyhose for each student and disperse them among the group so that everyone has the same amount and no one is left out.

376. Hold coins for field trips.

Not all school teachers fund field trips, but some do take on the expense of buying animal feed at the zoo, carousel rides at the park or tiny trinkets for the kids to bring home. If you're one of those teachers, put a few coins or tokens in the foot of your old hose to bring on field trips.

377. Clean bus lights.

If you're on a field trip in the winter, you may need to clean the head- and taillights of the bus en route. Road dirt and salt from the plows tend to cover them and make it hard for the bus driver to see and for other drivers to see the bus. Take the leg of your old hose and wet it with glass cleaner or snow to clean the bus lights as needed. It's always better to be safe than sorry, especially when caring for youngsters.

378. Store chalk.

How many times have you "lost" your chalk? Kids love to use chalk and some like to hide it from the teacher. I can't tell you how many minutes of class have been wasted because a teacher has to scramble around trying to find a bit of chalk. Keep your chalk in the foot of your old hose and hang it up high or hide it in a locked desk drawer so that your students don't lose any precious class time. That is why they are there, right?

379. Collect pinecones.

Fall projects can make for a fun-filled afternoon. Take your class outside and ask them to collect pinecones and pretty leaves to make a collage. Give each child a leg from an old pair of pantyhose to keep their findings in.

380. Make reindeer feed bags.

There is a nursery down the road from us that gives each child a sack of reindeer food when they come to buy a Christmas tree. My daughter takes hers and spreads it on my parent's lawn so that Rudolph and the gang can have a little snack when they arrive. Teachers are always looking for neat ways to give each child a little something during the holidays and this is it! Put some birdseed in the foot of your old hose and tie it with a pretty holiday ribbon and give one to each child before Christmas vacation.

381. Make candy bags for an Easter egg hunt.

My daughter's preschool holds a little Easter egg hunt for the kids every year. The wrapped chocolate eggs often get lost in the grass or stepped on. Try wrapping a few eggs in the foot of your old pantyhose and tie the bundles with pastel ribbon.

382. Make a sack for a scavenger hunt.

Kids love scavenger hunts because they get to solve little mysteries. My daughter makes lists every day and goes on her own little hunts! Cut the legs off of your old pantyhose and give one to each of your students so that they have a handy sack to put their trinkets in once they find them.

383. Tie around diplomas.

Every graduate, even a preschooler, deserves a diploma!
Make your next class diplomas special by tying a strip of
pantyhose around them.

384. Tie around award certificates.

When I was in 6th grade, there was a bully in my class.
One afternoon, he threw me against a bookcase and chased
me around the classroom. I don't know what got into me,
but I quickly decided that this would be his last hurrah and
I slammed my clogs down on his hands and broke five of
his knuckles. Then I ran for my life! My teacher, Mrs.
Magee, was so happy that someone finally stood up to this
bully that she gave me an award the following day. Wouldn't
it have been nice if my "bully" award had been rolled with
a nice strip of pantyhose?

385. Store erasers.

The kids in my grammar school used to bang the erasers
and get chalk dust all over everything. My teachers would
get so mad! Store your erasers in the leg of your old pantyhose and hang them up high so that your kids can't reach
them and make a mess of your classroom.

Chapter 8.

Wedding, Holiday, and Everyday Crafts

Every day is an extraordinary day when you have a few pairs of pantyhose on hand and a bright idea. There's no limit to what you can make when you incorporate the materials you have lying around your house. From catnip toys to holiday ornaments to elegant wedding favors—you'll never be bored!

386. Make potpourri sachets.

It's often hard to find the right material to hold loose or homemade potpourri. Many materials, such as tulle, have holes that will allow the small pieces to fall through and make a mess in your drawer. Although you want your lingerie to smell nice, you don't want the potpourri sitting in your panties! The feet of your old pantyhose are perfect for storing potpourri. Cut the feet of off an old pair of pantyhose, fill with potpourri, and tie with a satin ribbon. The hose will keep the potpourri contained while allowing the wonderful smell to filter out into your drawers.

387. Make scarecrows for fall decorating.

People are always looking for new ways to decorate their homes for each season, and fall can be especially hard. Many people buy mums and pumpkins, but neither of them last more than a few weeks if you have squirrels! Take two pairs of old pantyhose, stuff them, and attach them at the waists to form the body, legs, and arms. Stuff the seat of a third pair and use that for the head. You can then dress the scarecrow in some old jeans and a shirt and attach it to a stake. Your scarecrow will not only look great, but may chase some crows away too!

388. Make a camera case.

If you can't find your camera case and you want to protect your camera from getting knocked around in your bag or accidentally dropped, put it in the foot of your pantyhose. Layer another few feet of hose over that one if you want to take extra caution and tie a knot at the end of all the layers.

389. Make Christmas gift ornaments.

Find or buy a few little jewelry gift boxes. Use a strip of colored pantyhose to wrap around each box like a ribbon. Tie at the top, leaving a loop so you can hang the little gift on a tree branch. If you want to add more color, paint the box red or green before you begin.

390. Hold snacks for Christmas carolers.

Make treats to hand out to the Christmas carolers that come to your house to show them some holiday cheer and appreciation. Drop a few wrapped chocolate balls into the foot of your clean pantyhose, or wrap some Christmas cookies in plastic wrap before placing them in the foot of your hose, and tie with a festive ribbon. If you really want to make those carolers sing, serve them some hot cocoa with their treats. They may be in a hurry, so put the cocoa in paper cups and give them a candy or cookie bundle to go!

391. Make a cat toy.

Next time your cat destroys an expensive toy, make another one with the leg of your old hose. Simply cut a section from the leg, fill with catnip, and tie a tight knot at the top.

392. Block drafts.

With heating costs on the rise, every homeowner is looking for ways to conserve in the fall and winter. Heat can escape through closed windows and doors, so you need to stop those drafts from coming into your house. Draft blockers can cost up to $30.00 each at the stores, which is a lot of money when you can make them yourself for free. Cut the legs off of an old pair of pantyhose and stuff them with sand or several other pairs of pantyhose. Place them in front of doors and windows to keep heat inside your home. As my father always says, "We don't pay to heat the outside!"

393. Mark your luggage.

Wrap a strip of colorful pantyhose around the handle of your luggage so you can easily recognize it as it comes around the baggage claim carousel.

394. Make a throw toy for a dog.

Many dogs, especially puppies, are quite playful and love to play "chase." Making a throw toy out of old pantyhose couldn't be easier! Cut the leg from your old hose and tie several knots in it so that your dog has something to grab onto with his paws or teeth. You can even place a squeaky toy inside to add a little excitement to the game!

395. Fill with rocks and use as a paperweight.

Do your kids love to collect rocks? If so, I bet that you'd appreciate a good way to make use of them! Take a handful of rocks and tie them up in the foot of your old pantyhose with a nice ribbon to make a paperweight.

396. Wrap scented votive candles and keep in the linen closet.

My dad always tells me that I have the best-smelling towels! Not only do I dry them with two dryer sheets, but I also hide votive candles in and around the sheets and towels on the shelf. You don't want color rubbing off or bits of candle wax on your linens, so place the unwrapped votives in the foot of your pantyhose and tie at the top before placing them in the linen closet.

397. Fill scented soaps for your underwear drawer.

The scent of potpourri can be too strong for many people, and potpourri can be messy to work with. If you aren't a potpourri fan, try using scented soaps to freshen your lingerie drawer. Scented soaps come in a variety of wonderful fragrances, ranging from apple blossom to vanilla, and they can be quite mild. Placing a bar of scented soap in the foot of your old pantyhose and tying it with a pretty ribbon can be just enough to scent a dresser drawer.

398. Wrap a chocolate truffle for a place card.

It's often mind-boggling to try to find appropriate place cards for a dinner party. There is a broad range, which includes everything from ceramic flowers to photo frames, but you don't want to go overboard. Wrapping a delicious truffle in the foot of your clean white hose and tying it with a silk ribbon will not only look beautiful on your table, but will provide your guests with a scrumptious treat after dinner.

399. Tie as a ribbon around gifts.

If you're like me, you always discover that you're out of ribbon when the gift is wrapped and you're already late for the party. The great thing about using pantyhose to tie around a gift is that they'll always go with the paper that you choose. White hose for baby showers, weddings, and christenings; neutral hose for any occasion, and black for 40th birthday parties!

400. Hang wind chimes.

The sound of wind chimes can be very soothing when they're blown gently by the wind. Most wind chimes are hung either by a wire or a small hook, neither of which can withstand a big gust of wind. The leg of your pantyhose can be used to secure a set of wind chimes. Wrap the hose around the hook on top of the chimes several times and then tie a knot before hanging them on a hook or nail.

401. Stuff with lavender and make a sleep pillow.

Have you ever stayed overnight at a quaint bed and break-fast? They all seem to fill their guest rooms with the smell of lavender to aid you in your relaxation. You can create a similar experience by stuffing the leg of your pantyhose with lavender and stitching it up to make a pillow.

402. Make a wreath base.

Store-bought wreaths are expensive, and fresh wreaths don't last long. You can easily make your own wreaths with either fresh or faux berries and leaves. Cut the leg from an old pair of neutral pantyhose, stuff it with the rest of the hose, and tie to form a circle. You can apply berries, leaves, and fruit with a glue gun to make a beautiful accent for your front door.

403. Lengthen a ceiling fan or ceiling light cord.

To put the hanging cord in reach of shorter adults, attach a pantyhose leg or two to the end. Make sure it's not long enough to fall into the hands of a child.

404. Gather dog treats.

Whether you're on the go, or just trying to keep your kitchen tidy, keeping dog treats in the foot of an old pair of pantyhose will make either task easier.

405. Make a hemorrhoid pillow.

Unfortunately, hemorrhoids are a fact of life for many people. Hemorrhoids are painful and irritating, and they need to be tended to frequently. The last thing you want to do when you have a hemorrhoid is to neglect it. From what I've heard, sitting can be extremely uncomfortable when you have a hemorrhoid. A nice, soft pillow can help ease your discomfort when sitting. To make a hemorrhoid pillow, cut the leg of your pantyhose, stuff it with the remaining hose, and sew the ends together to form a circle. You can use the pillow at home, work, and even in the car.

406. Make a Christmas stocking.

Here's a fun project to help get you in the Christmas spirit! These stockings can be made for kids, pets, or as little gifts for the host or hostess of a dinner party. Cut the leg off your pantyhose and use a glue gun to trim the stocking with faux fur, felt decorations, and even holly leaves and berries. Once the stocking is decorated, fill it with candy!

407. Make streamers for a party.

Hanging streamers in a doorway can make the perfect entrance for any party. Cut your pantyhose into strips and hang in the doorway with tacks or tape.

408. Make scented Christmas pillows.

One of my favorite Christmas decorations is a little pillow stuffed with balsam. I love getting it out every year because it fills our living room with the wonderful smell of pine. To make a pillow, simply cut off the foot of your pantyhose, fill with balsam, tie a knot at the top, and then add some colorful ribbon, such as red and green plaid taffeta. You'll have it for years to come!

409. Wrap a bridal bouquet.

Today's brides have their bouquets tied up with ribbon or tulle. Instead of paying your florist to wrap the stems, wrap them yourself with white hose. As my father told me the day of my wedding, when my flowers needed fixing, "you are the only one who will know." As always, he was right!

410. Fill with Jordan almonds for a wedding favor.

The thought of putting together a wedding favor can often be too much for a busy bride to think about. You can make a nice, simple, edible parting gift for wedding guests by putting some Jordan almonds in the foot of your clean white pantyhose and tying it up with some silk ribbon. It's easy, and you can make the task fun by recruiting your bridesmaids to help you one afternoon!

411. Hang indoor plants.

Have you ever had a plant hanger break under the weight of a heavy hanging basket? It can happen in your living room when your plant becomes too heavy for the little plastic hanger that came with the pot. What a mess! Pantyhose won't break and will blend in with your décor if you use colored hose. Cut the legs from three pairs of pantyhose and use as many as needed to hang your plants.

412. Wrap gift baskets.

Gift baskets make great gifts, because you can fill them with a variety of items and the recipients will appreciate all the thought you put into them. It's so much fun to fill a big basket with gifts pertaining to a certain theme. I've given ski baskets at Christmas time, beach baskets in the summer, and harvest baskets in the fall. The hardest part of giving a gift basket is wrapping it! I used to buy big sheets of cellophane to wrap the gift baskets, but cellophane is hard to work with when you're wrapping an oddly shaped item. The leg from your pantyhose is much more flexible than cellophane, so it will easily stretch over a gift basket, and you can use any color, depending on the occasion. Add some sparkle to the package by tying a fancy ribbon to the top and attaching a nice gift card.

413. Hang pictures on the wall.

Picture wire can be difficult to work with because it's not very flexible and it's hard on your hands. Pantyhose are not only strong, they're soft and flexible. Cut the leg from an old pair of pantyhose and string through the hooks on the back of your picture to hang on the wall.

414. Make an exercise band.

Make an exercise band like the ones they use in Pilates classes by tying two pantyhose legs together in a circle. Lay on your side and place the band around both ankles. Lift the leg that's on top until you can feel it in your butt and thigh. You're doing the pantyhose workout!

415. Wrap an apple for a fall party favor.

There are so many wonderful fall flavors, and what better way to enjoy them than to share them with close friends? Hosting an intimate dinner party can be the perfect way to start the season off right, and giving your guests a little gift as they're leaving is a nice touch. Buy or make candied or caramel apples, wrap in the foot of your clean hose after they've cooled, and tie with an orange wired ribbon. It's a simple, but delicious, way to thank your guests for coming to your party. These would make great wedding favors too, depending on how many guests are attending.

416. Make St. Patrick's Day favors.

Throw a St. Patrick's Day party for all your friends and family and surprise them with a unique, pot of gold favor. Snip the feet off a few pairs of nude pantyhose and fill them with gold foil-wrapped chocolate coins. Tie the top into a knot and paint a green shamrock onto each little pot of gold. Your guests will be glad they came!

417. Wrap a pomander to keep the scent fresh.

A bowl of pomanders—oranges or apples covered with cloves—in the center of your dining-room table is a great focal point for any fall dinner party. As with any party, the more things you can prepare ahead of time, the more time you'll have to enjoy your guests. You can prepare the oranges or apples the day before your party and wrap them in the feet of your old pantyhose in order to keep their scent fresh. Unwrap the pomanders the day of your party and place in a pretty bowl to fill your dining room with the wonderful smell of cloves.

418. Make pillow tassels.

Adding decorative tassels can make any pillow look elegant. Cut little strips of pantyhose and sew them around the pillow edges. After the strips are sewn onto the pillow, tie a knot at the top of each one to give it a more finished look. For extra flair, adorn your tassels with a colored bead or jingle bell.

419. Hold price tags onto sale items.

Tag sales are a great way to unload things that you no longer want or need. If you're done having children, sell all of the baby things like swings and infant toys, and if you're not a cook, sell all the cookbooks people have given you in hopes of teaching you something. (I know this one from personal experience!) Attach big easy-to-read tags to each item with the name printed clearly so you can spend your time collecting money, not answering price questions. Buy the tags, or make them, with a hole in the top corner and attach them to your sale items with a strip of pantyhose.

420. Make a wig.

This is a great idea for Halloween! Use a shower cap as a base and sew little strips of pantyhose to it to make a funny wig.

421. Hold an old book together.

When my daughter was two, her favorite book was "Elmo's Valentine" and we read it several times a day. That book went everywhere with us! Eventually, the pages became frayed and the binding came off. Instead of throwing it out, I punched holes in the top left corner so we could tie the pages together. To prolong the life of a beloved book, thread a strip of pantyhose through the punched holes and tie it in a tight knot. Your child will love it just the same!

422. Dye Easter eggs.

Everyone dyes Easter eggs at one time or another and the dye kits are the same year after year. Add a new design to your eggs by putting them into the foot of your old pantyhose before dipping them in various colors. Make sure that you tie the egg and leave a long strip of pantyhose at the top so that you can lift the eggs out when they're done.

423. Wrap cut votive candles.

Candles are a great way to freshen up your lingerie drawer or linen closet, but all candles lose their scent after a while. To rejuvenate them, cut them in half to release the scent from inside the candle. After cutting the candles, put them in the foot of your pantyhose and tie at the top. This prevents the wax bits from getting all over your dresser drawer or closet shelves while allowing the scent to fill your home.

424. Tie a flag to your mailbox.

I like to put a little American flag on my mailbox each summer to add a patriotic flair to our driveway. Just wedging it between the mailbox and post doesn't keep it secure, so I tie it to the post with neutral pantyhose. Use white if that's the color of your mailbox. The flag is secure, even in windy weather, and the hose will blend right in.

425. Tie balloons to your mailbox.

Our driveway is somewhat hidden by trees so I like to mark it clearly when we have any kind of gathering. For my daughter's birthday party, I tie three or four balloons to the mailbox so guests can find their way. The thin string that comes tied to balloons is usually too weak to hold them securely. If you don't want the balloons working their way loose and floating away, try mounting them to the mailbox with a strip of pantyhose.

426. Make an Indian corn decoration.

Fall is one of the easiest seasons to decorate for! Throw a few pumpkins on your front steps with some richly colored mums, put a bale of hay on your porch and hang some Indian corn on your front door. After tying the three pieces of corn together with wire, use a neutral colored pantyhose strip to hang the corn from a nail on your front door. The neutral tone is just right for fall!

427. Make napkin rings.

If you're having a dinner party and setting a formal table, use pantyhose strips as napkin holders. Roll your linen napkins and tie them with a strip of pantyhose. You can use white, neutral or whatever color blends nicely with your napkins and dinner plates. If you want to spice them up a little bit, attach a silk flower to the front.

428. Make Christmas napkin rings.

The holiday season is filled with parties and if you're hosting one, this is for you. It's not necessary to give favors out at an adult party, but if you want to, do it practically. Roll your linen napkins, tie them with a strip of white pantyhose and tie in a pretty Christmas ornament on the top. This kills two birds with one stone, so to speak. First it serves as a napkin ring and secondly, it provides your guest with a nice and simple favor. Feliz Navidad!

429. Tie tote bag handles together.

Tote bags are great for every kind of trip. Whether you're headed to the beach or staying somewhere overnight, overpacking a tote bag is easy! My biggest tote bag has a zipper, thankfully, but many do not. If your tote bag is overstuffed, tie the handles together with pantyhose strips. Not only will the contents of your tote bag stay put but your bag will also be easier to carry.

430. Make bike streamers.

Kids love the feeling of importance that comes with riding their bike in the local parade. Add to their fun by making bike streamers out of your old colored pantyhose. Cut the pantyhose into strips and tie them to the handlebars of your child's bike so they have extra flair as they parade along.

431. Make flowers for a parade float.

I remember several people gathering in my parent's garage to decorate parade floats for homecoming and 4th of July parades. We used to use box, upon box, of Kleenex to make flowers for these floats. Not only was this incredibly time consuming, but it was costly! To save time and money, make pantyhose flowers from squares of pantyhose. The flowers will be much bigger, so you won't have to make as many, and they won't cost you a thing. Cut your pantyhose into squares. Pick up the center of the square and tie a knot at the bottom of the bloom. Attach a wire or pipe cleaner to the knot and mount to the float.

432. Line a basket.

If you want to dress up a basket, cut the leg from an old pair of pantyhose and stretch around the top of your basket. For added flair, glue some silk flowers or nice beads to the overhanging hose.

433. Decorate a pet collar.

Is it time for Fido to get a fashion refresh? Cut a strip of pantyhose from an old pair and wrap it around your dog or cat's collar. Tie a pretty bow for a girl dog or a bowtie for a boy.

434. Make afghan fringes.

Even if you're not a crafter, this is easy! Cut little strips of pantyhose, in any color that you like, and sew them onto an afghan. If you have several different colored pantyhose, you may want to alternate the colors as you go around.

435. Hang for vertical blinds.

Of course, these will not work as room darkening blinds, but they will provide a thin barrier between you and passersby. Cut your pantyhose into strips and neatly tie them to a curtain rod.

436. Tie purse straps together

Some of the cutest purses come without a zipper! I hate having an open purse and inviting all the world to see what I have inside, not to mention losing things when I bend over to get something. If you have a cute purse without a convenient closure, tie the two handles together with pantyhose strips to keep it closed.

437. Hang a mail basket on your house.

Hang a mail basket on the side of your house to replace the standard issue metal mailbox at the end of your driveway. Hang it from a nail on your front porch or front door using a strip of pantyhose. You'll want to mark it for incoming and outgoing mail—you don't want your mailman to be flustered!

438. Make a decorative soap wrapper.

Little accents often make regular items look extraordinary.
For example, take a scented bar of soap, wrap it in a strip of
your old pantyhose and tie the strip in place with a wired
ribbon. Tie the ends of the ribbon into a pretty bow and
allow the fresh scent to fill your bathroom. If you have a
guest bathroom in your home, put a few of these soaps in a
nice basket or dish on the side of the sink.

439. Tie guest towels together.

One way to make house guests feel welcome is to show
that you've planned for their arrival. Stack a bath towel,
hand towel and face cloth and then tie them together with
the leg of your old pantyhose. The foot should be cut off,
of course . . . after all, we don't want to give away all of
our secrets!

440. Make a chunky necklace.

Women today are wearing a lot of chunky and colorful
jewelry, especially in the summer months. To make a lovely
summer necklace, string some large, colorful beads on a
strip of white pantyhose. Cover the strip with beads, but
leave enough room at the top to tie a bow around your
neck. Ooh, la la!

441. Hang Christmas ornaments.

You may have some ornaments that have lost their hooks or you may have some heavy ornaments that need a lot of support. Either way, pantyhose can help. Cut your pantyhose legs into strips and tie them to every ornament that needs to be hung. You can even tie little bows at the top to make them look more festive.

442. Stuff a gift bag.

I'm sure that I'm not the only one who hates to use tissue paper. It rips and wrinkles before you even deliver the gift, not to mention the fact that it takes a whole package to actually fill a medium sized gift bag! Stuff a gift bag with pantyhose by cutting the hose into little strips and sprinkling them into the bag like confetti or by enveloping the gift in large sections of pantyhose as you would with tissue paper.

443. Make peds.

Stores like Marshall's and T.J. Maxx offer great deals on shoes, but they don't offer peds for trying them on. Peds keep other foot germs at bay, make it easier to get shoes on and off and give a real feel for how well a pair of shoes fit. To make your own, cut the feet off of an old pair of pantyhose and tuck them in your purse for impromptu shoe shopping trips.

444. Make a fanny pack.

This may not be suitable for people who are in and out of their fanny pack constantly, but it's great for people who want to store things just in case they need them. Cut the leg off of an old pair of pantyhose, put everyday necessities like Chapstick, money, and sunscreen inside and tie the hose around your waist to keep them all in reach.

445. Lengthen a lunch bag strap.

When I worked full-time before my daughter was born, I used to bring lunch to work with me. (I could never rely on the cafeteria's food to be good, much less enjoyable.) The problem with packing a lunch is you have to transport it to your office along with your purse, briefcase, coffee, and anything else you may be carrying. It's much easier to carry a lunch bag on your shoulder than it is to hold the strap in your hand. Use pantyhose to turn your lunch bag strap into a comfortable shoulder strap. One way is to remove the lunch bag strap altogether and replace it with the leg of your hose. The second way is to unbuckle one end of the strap, tie the pantyhose leg to the end of it and then thread the pantyhose through the buckle. It may not look great, but it will get the job done!

446. Make kitchen chair pads.

Chair pads not only add to your kitchen décor, but they make your chairs so much more comfortable. Find some fabric that blends nicely with your kitchen colors, cut two pieces for each chair pad that you'll be making, sew three-quarters around the fabric and stuff with your old pantyhose. After the cushions are stuffed, stitch them up to keep the stuffing inside.

447. Lengthen your purse strap.

The only purses that are comfortable on my shoulder are the ones from ten to fifteen years ago that are no longer in style. These purses had straps long enough to wear across your chest and then some! Now, the purse straps are so short that a lot of them don't even fit on my shoulder. The last thing I need is to have to hold my purse on my shoulder in addition to holding my daughter's hand and groceries all the while opening doors and loading the car. A solution to this problem is to lengthen your purse strap with a strip of pantyhose. No, it won't be as fashionable as the purse, but it will keep your hands free! Free one end of your purse strap and sew a length of pantyhose to the end of the strap. Attach the other end of the pantyhose to your purse by weaving it through a buckle, if there is one, or by sewing it securely in place.

448. Make a passport holder.

Slip your passport into the leg of your pantyhose and tie the pantyhose leg around your waist underneath your clothes. Whether you're waiting in line at the airport or sightseeing abroad, this will help keep your passport from being stolen or lost.

449. Tie on your finger as a reminder.

Was it Felix, or Oscar, from *The Odd Couple* who used to do this? Pantyhose strips are much stronger than string and you won't be able to miss one when it's tied to your finger!

450. Tie your grocery list to your shopping cart.

Don't let that list slip through the slats of the cart again! Poke a hole at the top of your grocery list and use a strip of hose to tie it to the cart where you can easily see it as you shop.

451. Tie chair pads to kitchen chairs.

After you've made the cushions for your kitchen chairs, sew pantyhose strips, four per cushion, to the back of the cushions and tie around the backs of your chairs. Make sure that you tie the cushions loosely enough so that there is a little give when people sit down. The pantyhose ties will hold up better than the cotton ties that always seem to rip over time.

452. Wrap gifts.

I have seen everything from funnies to pillowcases, so why not pantyhose? You can make the wrapping as simple or as fancy as you'd like.

453. Make a temporary fan belt for your car.

Yes, it really works! If your fan belt breaks and you need to keep driving, take a pair of pantyhose and twist it into a long rope. Carefully thread it around the pulleys on the car's engine and water pump. Pull it tight and tie a knot. Get thee to a mechanic right away!

454. Hang jingle bells on your front door.

I really get into Christmas and love decorating my home for the holidays. There are lots of inexpensive Christmas decorations to choose from and many are easy to put up. Remember, a little sparkle goes a long way! Tie some jingle bells to your front door with a strip of pantyhose. The bells will both announce family members as they arrive home and welcome guests to a holiday party.

455. Make a wine bag.

A bottle of wine makes a great hostess gift for any party. Use the leg of your old pantyhose as a wine bag and tie a pretty ribbon around the top for a stunning presentation of your party gift.

456. Make a pearl necklace.

If you are a traditional woman, at least jewelry wise, you can make a beautiful faux pearl necklace with a thin strip of white pantyhose and some white pearl beads. Simply string the pearls onto the pantyhose and tie around your neck.

457. Make a pearl bracelet.

Every necklace should have a matching bracelet, right?

458. Make a kissing ball.

Rekindle the romance around the holidays! Stuff the foot of your pantyhose with some mistletoe, tie the top and hang above a doorway that your honey frequently passes through. You can also decorate the outside of the kissing ball with mistletoe and holly and tie a pretty red ribbon around the top.

459. Make hand warmers.

If you have children, you probably spend a great deal of time enjoying the winter weather! My mother always told me to wear layers to keep warm and, as much of a pain as it is, she was right. I feel the cold first in my hands, even with gloves on. Putting an extra layer on your hands can make all the difference, especially when you're up to your elbows in a snow mountain. Cut the feet off of your old pantyhose and wear them on your hands under your mittens.

460. Make snow for your Christmas village.

Some people put out a little Christmas village every year for decoration. You can buy fake snow to lay under the village, but why bother when all you need is pantyhose! Find a pair of white pantyhose and cut a big square of "snow" to place under the houses and shops in your Christmas village.

461. Make balsam ornaments for an artificial Christmas tree.

Do you love the smell of a real Christmas tree, but hate the mess it makes? Pantyhose can help! Invest in a realistic-looking, artificial Christmas tree. Department stores sell cans of the tree smell you love, but the scent won't last long and you'll have to spend the holiday season walking around with a spray bottle. Fill the feet of your old pantyhose with balsam and tie at the top with a pretty red, green or gold ribbon. Make a loop at the top and hang several of these ornaments on your artificial tree. No one will suspect that it's a fake!

462. Tie around a vase of flowers.

If you've ever had flowers delivered from the florist, you probably admired the beautiful ribbon that came tied around the vase. The next time you're arranging fresh flowers from your garden, or the store, tie a pretty bow around the vase with the leg of your white pantyhose.

463. Make a cell phone holder.

It's always good to protect your cell phone from scratches and falls, especially since buying a new one can cost a small fortune! For an impromptu cell phone holder, drop your phone into the foot of your old pantyhose and tie closed. Add a few more layers of hose for extra protection. Keep it in your pocket or purse or tie to your belt and rest assured that it's protected.

464. Decorate a hat.

If you like to wear hats or if you're going to a summer wedding, add a little flare to your brim with a strip of pantyhose tied in a bow or a knot. You can work in a sprig of leaves or a pretty silk flower too!

465. Create cookie or cake decorations.

Put candy canes or peppermint candies into the foot of your old hose and then roll it with a rolling pin to crush for cake or cookie decorations.

466. Hang a shower curtain.

Tying pantyhose strips around a shower rod is much easier and quicker than fussing with the little button holes on the curtain!

467. Make a window draft blocker.

Our house is drafty. We've tried everything from taping plastic on our windows (not very attractive) to using adhesive insulation strips, which don't come off easily, on every sill. Nothing works like a draft blocker, but they can be hard to find. You can easily make your own by stuffing a long pocket of fabric with your old pantyhose. You can make it as long and as thick as you want, depending on your window sizes.

468. Decorate a scrapbook.

Lots of people are into scrapbooking these days. What better way to add texture to a scrapbook page than to include a few pieces of pantyhose. Cut them into shapes that follow your theme. For instance, cut out the shape of a lighthouse for a page documenting your ocean side vacation.

469. Wrap decorative Easter eggs for gifts.

I love dying Easter eggs and turning them into little works of art! I know several crafty people who blow out the eggs so they can paint and display them for the spring holiday. These beautiful eggs would be a nice gift to bring to the hostess of an Easter brunch or to guests coming to have Easter dinner at your house. Wrap the delicate eggs gently in a section of white pantyhose and tie with a pretty spring ribbon.

470. Wrap a candle for a bridal shower favor.

I have seen everything when it comes to favors!
Unfortunately, the people giving out favors aren't always
thinking of what guests might find most useful. For example,
I have no use for a gaudy, plastic jewelry box! For my sister's
shower, I ordered votive candles from Yankee Candle that
blended nicely with her flowers. As an added bonus, the
scent on the wrapper was personalized with her name! I
then wrapped the candles in pretty white pantyhose and
tied with an embossed card and silk ribbon. It was quick,
easy and the guests loved them.

471. Tie back your curtains.

I love having curtains that I can close at night, but I need to
let the light in during the day. This is easy when you can
use the legs from your old pantyhose to tie your curtains
back and out of way when the sun is shining.

472. Tie sections of valances.

I love window treatments and valances are my favorite!
Valances work well because they are up and out of the way
and they allow the light to come right on in. Some valances
are a little long and need to be divided somehow. The legs
of your old hose will do fine! Stretch a section of hose and
tie behind the valance so no one will see your handy work.

473. Make a flag for your boat.

If you put a lot of love and time into your boat, why not adorn her mast with a flag. Cut the leg off an old pair of pantyhose and cut the foot off the end. Paint it with stripes or polka-dots, attach it to the mast and fly it like a windsock.

474. Make streamers for a party entrance.

This is a great idea for reunions, costume parties, and any kind of party that would lend itself to an entrance of streamers. The easiest way to do it is to cut strips of pantyhose and tack them around a doorway or entryway so that they flutter every time a guest breezes in.

475. Decorate a bride and groom's car.

Streamers tend to rip and blow away as you're driving down the road of marital bliss. Cut the legs from your white pantyhose and tie them tightly to the inside of the trunk so they stay on for the long haul! You can also tie short pantyhose strips to the car's hubcaps so they make a more dramatic departure.

476. Make small dog leash.

Now, this won't work for any dog that's bigger than a cat! Attach the end of a pantyhose leg securely to their collar and hold the foot.

477. Make a dog bed.

Dogs love to sleep on human beds, right? If you're like me, you sleep in the same position so the DOG stays comfortable. Give your dog the old heave ho and make him a comfortable bed of his own! Pick out a fabric that's suitable for a dog and sew it into any shape that you'd like. Leave a section open so that you can stuff the bed with your old pantyhose and then stitch it closed. Show the dog his new bed and put his favorite chew toy on it to draw him over onto it.

478. Pick up doggy waste when walking your dog.

Stuff several legs of pantyhose into your pocket before you take your dog on a walk. Take one out each time you need to scoop up their mess—you may want to put one leg inside another so you can keep a comfortable distance.

479. Cover a book.

You can do anything with a blank canvas! Stretch the seat of your old pantyhose over a favorite book or notebook and secure with heavy-duty tape. Cover the seam and add some flair by applying beads, letters, flowers, and even sequins and glitter to your nylon book cover. If you want to personalize it even more, glue a picture of someone special, or a someplace special, to the front.

480. Make into a stress ball.

I've probably received a stress ball at every job I've ever had! My bosses would tell me that it was a little gift, a token of appreciation, but did everyone get them? Hmmm. Stress balls are great for the busy business person juggling the pressures of work and home, as well as for the stay-at-home parent who spends his/her day negotiating, bribing, and trying to rationalize with a child. If you fall into one of these categories, go cut the foot off of your old pantyhose, fill it with some rubber or squishy material like silly putty and tie a knot at the top. Whenever you feel stressed, and can't walk away for ten minutes, clench this as tightly as you possiblly can!

481. Dust hard-to-reach places.

Tie pantyhose legs to telescoping pole to dust high ceilings and ceiling fans.

482. Make birdseed bags for wedding guests.

If you'd like to give your guests something to throw at you after you've become man and wife, birdseed is the politically correct choice these days. Who knew that birds couldn't eat rice? Fill the feet of your white pantyhose with birdseed and tie them with a pretty ribbon that matches the color of your wedding party. Display the bags in a fancy basket next to your guest book if you are not having ushers. If you are having ushers, ask them to give one birdseed bag to each guest as they are seated.

483. Make roping for a sailing party.

It's easy to decorate for a nautical themed party with blue and white pantyhose. Simply braid them together to make rope and drape it around the edges of a table or along the wall for visual interest.

484. Tie cans to a newlywed getaway car.

Your friends may hate you, but you want to make sure that they get the appropriate amount of attention!

Chapter 9.

Wacky and Wild

Some of you may think that the majority of the ideas in this book are pretty wacky, but you ain't seen nothing yet! I've saved the best for last—the following ideas are not for the faint of heart! From pet hammocks to knee braces, there's no stopping the power of pantyhose.

485. Make a cat leash.

Now, I don't walk my cat, but I have seen people taking their kitties for a stroll. You can easily make a leash for your cat by cutting the leg off an old pair of pantyhose. Make sure that your cat is wearing a comfortable collar and tie one end of the strip to the collar. Hold the other end in your hand to keep your cat from running off. This is especially important if your cat hasn't spent a lot of time outside.

486. Make a hamster hammock.

This does sound ridiculous, I know, but hamsters don't actually lounge in the hammock, they just use it to exercise! What else do they have to do in that cage? To make a hamster hammock, tie the leg of your pantyhose to either side of the cage and watch the hamster climb and flip and have a great time.

487. Make a hat.

I know this may sound crazy, but you can make a cute fall or winter hat by using the seat of your old pantyhose. Cut the seat from a neutral pair of pantyhose and check that the waistband fits snugly on your head. Tie a knot at the top so you have the general form of a hat. Once the form is made, sew little pieces of fleece to the outside of your hat. Use different colors to make an interesting patchwork design. Be sure to really fill it in so that you can't see the pantyhose underneath.

488. Make a cat pillow.

Stuff the seat of your old hose with some foam to make a pillow for your cat to sleep on. Your cat will love to sink right into it!

489. Wrap a glass or light bulb for a Jewish wedding ceremony.

Now, I don't know if this is kosher, but it seemed like a good idea to me! Wrap a glass or light bulb in the foot of your hose and tie with a white silk ribbon to dress it up. This way the pieces won't go everywhere when you stomp on it.

490. Make a tourniquet.

In the event that you are severely injured, or are with someone who is, and are unable to control the bleeding, use the leg of your old pantyhose as a tourniquet. Campers may want to take note and pack a few legs in their backpack just in case of emergency!

491. Make an arm sling.

The first thing a nurse will do when a patient has an injured arm is to cradle it in a sling to alleviate the pressure. If you get an arm injury and can't get to a hospital right away, make a sling with the leg of your old pantyhose.

492. Wrap the handles of your crutches.

When I was 13 years old, I tore all the ligaments in my knee and was on crutches for two weeks. Ouch! I remember getting blisters on my hands from leaning on the hard wooden handles of my crutches for so long. If you ever need to use a crutch, wrap the handle with the leg of your pantyhose first in order to protect your hands.

493. Elevate an injured leg.

This is especially important when you are sleeping! Most people can't control their sleep movements but you need to sleep somewhat still if you have been injured. To sleep without putting much pressure on your leg, create a sling from your old pantyhose and use it to elevate your leg. You may have to attach the ends of the sling to the ceiling or your bed frame for support.

494. Warm your gear shift.

My car gets so cold in the winter, so every little bit helps! Cut off the bottom half of a pantyhose leg and place it over your gear shift.

495. Blow your nose in emergencies.

I know this sounds gross, but it's better than wiping it on your sleeve! Store a few sections in your purse and in your car in case you run out of Kleenex.

496. Hang fuzzy dice to your rearview mirror.

I have wanted a Corvette for as long as I can remember. When I was younger, I wanted a new model, red of course, with a pair of fuzzy dice hanging above the dash. Now, that I am older and my taste has improved, I dream of owning a '57 Corvette convertible, still red but no fuzzy dice. If you are still in the "fuzzy dice" stage, you can hang your dice with a strip of your old pantyhose. The pantyhose can lengthen the ties, thereby making the dice hang lower so they won't block your vision.

497. Tie sheet music to your arm or instrument for a parade.

I grew up in a town that has parades for everything! I also have a family full of musicians who like to march in the 4th of July and Memorial Day parades. If you are a musician and you need a way to keep your eye on the music notes while you're marching, tie your sheet music to your arm with a strip of pantyhose.

498. Substitute for toilet paper in an emergency.

You never know what kind of situation you'll end up in if your car breaks down or you're camping out in the woods. It might be a good idea to store a few squares of pantyhose in your car or keep some in your pocket if you're camping.

499. Make a knee brace.

Because of an old knee injury, I have to wear knee support when taking part in sports. Unless you need a medical brace, you can simply wrap your knee tightly in pantyhose to give it some extra support. Make sure that you wrap above and below the knee so that the entire area is covered.

500. Make a promise ring.

If you don't have any money to buy a ring, or if you have an emergency situation and the only thing you have handy is a pair of pantyhose, then cut a little strip of pantyhose (preferably white) and tie it around your beloved's finger in a bow. Love is blind, right?